I0119754

William Archer Purrington

A Review of Recent Legal Decisions

Affecting physicians, dentists, druggists and the public health, together

with a brief for the prosecution of unlicensed practitioners of medicine,

dentistry, or pharmacy - Vol. 1

William Archer Purrington

A Review of Recent Legal Decisions
*Affecting physicians, dentists, druggists and the public health, together with a brief
for the prosecution of unlicensed practitioners of medicine, dentistry, or pharmacy -
Vol. 1*

ISBN/EAN: 9783337369934

Printed in Europe, USA, Canada, Australia, Japan

Cover: Foto ©Suzi / pixelio.de

More available books at **www.hansebooks.com**

A REVIEW OF RECENT

LEGAL DECISIONS

AFFECTING

PHYSICIANS, DENTISTS, DRUGGISTS

AND THE

PUBLIC HEALTH

TOGETHER WITH

A BRIEF

FOR THE PROSECUTION OF UNLICENSED PRACTITIONERS
OF MEDICINE, DENTISTRY, OR PHARMACY, WITH
A PAPER UPON MANSLAUGHTER, CHRIS-
TIAN SCIENCE AND THE LAW
AND OTHER MATTER

By W. A. PURRINGTON

OF THE NEW YORK BAR

Counsel of the Dental Society of the State of New York, and Lecturer of Medical and
Dental Jurisprudence in the New York College of Dentistry, and one of the
collaborators in "A System of Legal Medicine," by Allan
McLane Hamilton, and others, etc.

NEW YORK

E. B. TREAT & COMPANY

241-243 West 23d Street

1899

PREFATORY.

FORMERLY, reported law cases specifically affecting medical practitioners were comparatively rare. In his work on "The Jurisprudence of Medicine," published in 1869, Ordronaux cited 324. In 1871, Glenn's "Treatise upon Laws Affecting Medical Men" cited but 438. In 1877, McClelland, in his "Civil Malpractice," collected but 76; in that work, however, cases are reported in full instead of being merely cited. In "The Law and Medical Men," published in 1884 by Mr. Vashan Rogers, 334 cases are cited, and in Field's "Medico-Legal Guide," appearing in 1887, there are 410 citations. Since that time, owing to increasing medical legislation and litigation of malpractice actions, the number of cases reported annually is much greater than ever before. In the single article upon "The Legal Relations of Physicians and Surgeons to their Patients and to One Another," in "A System of Legal Medicine," by Allan McLane Hamilton and others, published in 1894, there are 518 cases cited, and in "The International Medical Annual" for 1898 the number of such law cases noted for the preceding year was 131.

The publishers of that Annual have therefore thought it worth while to issue its review of legal decisions during the past year as a separate pamphlet, adding to it a convenient brief of the law points that usually arise in the prosecution of unlicensed practitioners of Medicine, Dentistry, and Pharmacy, and such other matter as may serve to make clear the public purpose and benefit of the laws regulating the practice of these vocations.

The brief, it is believed, gives citations of authority upon any points likely to arise in such prosecutions, sufficient to make it of assistance at trial to magistrates, courts, and counsel; and it is hoped that the other text may be serviceable in pointing out the true purpose of medical legislation, and persuading those who have thought little of the matter, that dentistry is not a trade or a handicraft or yet a profession apart, as some have contended, but is a specialty of medicine.

The laws of the various States have not been reprinted because their bulk would increase the size and cost of the pamphlet to an extent not compensated for by the occasional advantage to the reader of having at hand the statute of some State other than his own, and also because these laws, being still in formative process, are so often amended that a compilation correct when given to the printer might be defective upon issuing from the press.

It is a pleasure in this connection to give public recognition to the untiring zeal of my friend, Dr. William Carr, of New York city, who as censor of the First District Dental Society, chairman of the Law Committee of the Dental Society of the State of New York, member of the State Board of Dental Examiners, trustee of the New York College of Dentistry, and in other capacities has for years freely devoted his time and means to the advancement of the standard of professional education in the special department of medical science wherein he elected to practise after graduation as a Doctor of Medicine, thus fully paying the debt that every one is said to owe to his profession.

I have added the article upon Manslaughter, Christian Science, and the Law, reprinted from the *Medical Record*, with footnotes calling attention to cases on the brief in this pamphlet, correcting the citation of Regina *v.* Cook, which should have been Regina *v.* Senior, and citing the decision in the latter case, reported after that article went to press. The increase in the number of so-called Christian Scientists, and the prevalent ignorance, even among the votaries of the cult, of what its theories are, led me to write, at the request of the editor, for the March number of the *North American Review*, an article summarizing the teachings of Mrs. Eddy and discussing their legal aspects. It is quite safe to say, judging from the testimony in reported law cases, that no two practitioners of Christian Science would probably agree with themselves or their founder as to what the theory and the practice of the cult are.

W. A. PURRINGTON.

59 WALL STREET, April 10, 1899.

CONTENTS.

NOTES OF AMERICAN LEGAL DECISIONS.

[From advance sheets, *International Medical Annual.*]

A REVIEW OF CASES AFFECTING MEDICAL MEN.

The Purpose and Justification of Medical Laws.

By the term "medical laws" is here meant all legislative acts regulating the practice of either general physic and surgery, or special departments thereof, as dentistry and pharmacy.

The right of every man to the fullest opportunity consistent with public welfare of earning a livelihood by exercising whatever talents and aptitudes for industry he may have, is so manifest and vital that every proposition to restrain it is properly looked upon with jealous scrutiny.

Laws framed only to benefit a class at the expense of the community, by placing any handicraft, art, calling, or business in the hands of the few to their enrichment, and so diminishing competition, are indefensible, injurious to the State, and obstructive to progress in the art, profession, or science affected.

The prescription by law of formulas or methods of practice, the statutory fostering of one system at the expense of another in any liberal calling, are improper uses of legislation. In medicine, for instance, it would be unwise to forbid absolutely the practice of any particular method of cure, or to command that no treatment of the sick should be followed unless approved by the regular practitioners; but it seems entirely proper to forbid the uneducated to practise according to any system. In other words, although the State, in order to protect private citizens and the public health against ignorance and imposture, may wisely require, as a prerequisite of license to practise medicine at all, a general education supplemented by special medical study and knowledge, yet it would be most unwise, and obstructive to progress, should the system or methods of practice be prescribed by statute, or the practice of any system absolutely forbidden. When the licentiate has demonstrated that he is adequately equipped for his profession by study and acquirement, according to the learning of the age, he should be left free to apply his knowledge, skill, and judgment in particular cases, to investigate and experiment. His education and the judgment of his fellows afford the best safeguard against his adoption of mere vagaries; while civil and criminal liability for malpractice, the sense of duty, and desire to succeed professionally afford in each case the best assurances that he will exercise due caution and requisite care.

The right of the State, having in view the public welfare, to regulate by general laws the practice of medicine, has often been discussed by courts of last resort, which have affirmed the constitutionality of such legislation, and approved its purpose. In the decisive case of Dent v. State of West Virginia (129 U. S. 114), Mr. Justice Field, expressing the unanimous opinion of the Supreme Court of the United States, said: "Few professions require more careful preparation by one who seeks to enter it than that of medicine. It has to deal with all those subtle and mysterious influences upon which health and life depend; and requires not only a knowledge of the properties of vegetable and mineral substances, but of the human body in all its complicated parts, and their relation to each other, as well as their influence upon the mind. The physician must be able to detect readily the presence of disease, and prescribe appropriate remedies for its removal. Every one may have occasion to consult him, but comparatively few can judge of the qualifications of learning and skill which he possesses. Reliance must be placed upon the assurance given by his license, issued by an authority competent to judge in that respect, that he possesses the requisite qualifications. Due consideration, therefore, for the protection of society may well induce the State to exclude from practice those who have not such a license, or who are found upon examination not to be fully qualified."

From remote times the practice of medicine has been regulated by law, to greater or less extent, with occasional intervals when selfish class effort, actual or supposed, to use for private gain the public statute, has brought about reaction,—as when the House of Lords, reversing the law courts in the case of

Rose *v.* The College of Physicians (3 Salk., 17; 6 Mod., 44; 5 Bro. Parl. Rep., 553; A.D. 1703), and deciding that apothecaries as well as physicians might prescribe drugs, made the apothecary the general medical practitioner of England; a decision arrived at for the reason, apparently, that their lordships considered it overburdensome to require the poor, for themselves, and the rich, for their servants, to call in a physician to prescribe, an apothecary to dispense, and a surgeon to let blood.*

The old English statutes quaintly express both the justification of and objection to medical legislation, from the viewpoint of public welfare; thus the Act of Parliament of 1540, consolidating the separate mysteries of the barbers and surgeons, recited that persons using the mystery of surgery took into their houses people infected with pestilence, great pox, and other contagious infirmities, and also exercised barbery, as washing, shaving, or other feats thereto belonging, which was very perilous for infecting the King's liege people. So, too, the Faculty of Physicians and Surgeons of Glasgow was established in 1599 to avoid the inconvenience caused by "ignorant, unskilled, and unlearned persons, who under the color of chirurgeons are in the habit of abusing the people to their pleasure, and of destroying thereby infinite numbers of his Majesty's subjects." The first medical act of Henry VIII.† recited that physic and surgery were practised by "ignorant persons who could tell no letters on the book, common artificers, smiths, weavers, and women who took upon themselves great cures, partly using sorcery and witchcraft, and partly applying very noxious medicines to the disease"; and subsequently in the same reign,‡ medical practice was confined to physicians and surgeons. On the other hand, later in that reign,§ for the alleged reason that the "Company and Fellowships of Surgeons in London, minding only their own lucres, and nothing the profit or ease of the diseased or patient, have sued, troubled, and vexed divers honest persons, etc., . . . and it is now well known that the surgeons admitted will do no cure to any per-

* "Evolution of the Apothecary," *Medical Record*, September 11th, 1886, vol. xxx., p. 281.
† 3 Hen. VIII., c. 11, (A.D. 1511.)
‡ 14 and 15 Hen. VIII., c. v.; 32 Hen. VIII., c. xl.
§ 34 and 35 Hen. VIII., c. viii.

son, but where they shall know to be rewarded, with a greater sum or reward than the cure extendeth unto," and further because, "although the most part of the persons of the said craft of surgery have small cunning, yet they will take great sums of money and do little therefor," it was permitted that persons with knowledge and experience of the nature of herbs might practise and minister them, and apply outward remedies without suit or vexation.*

So in New York at the beginning of the century the practice of medicine was strictly regulated, but later an exception was made in favor of persons using herbs of home growth, and subsequently the statutes forbidding practice by the unlicensed were entirely repealed, only to be restored eventually, so that to-day the requirements of license in that State and the penalties for unlawful practice are greater than they were under the early laws.

In this way has medical legislation been assailed and defended. But at all times its avowed purpose and sole justification have been the protection of the public against ignorant men undertaking to care for the sick without due knowledge of disease or its treatment.

Dentistry Is a Specialty of Medicine.

To-day in medical practice we approach the condition of the Egyptians, who had, as Herodotus writes,† special practitioners of medicine for every part of the body. Medical schools prepare students to begin professional life as general practitioners; the majority of physicians do so begin it, and from the necessities of the case the country doctor is quite certain to remain in general practice for life. But in great cities the tendency to specialism grows. Probably the best specialist is he who, spending his earlier years in general practice, confines himself later to a particular field into which he is led by circumstance or special interest and aptitudes. But whether one studies primarily to become, or becomes by the drift of circum-

---

* The old English statutes are collected by Glenn, " Laws Affecting Medical Men," and are recited less fully in Mr. Vashan Rogers' very entertaining book, " The Law and Medical Men."

† Euterpe, § 84.

stances, an otologist, ophthalmologist, orthopedist, gynecologist, laryngologist, odontologist or dentist, dermatologist, or what not, the fact that he devotes himself exclusively to a special region of the human body does not render it unnecessary, but rather the contrary, that he should found his specialization upon a knowledge of general principles; nor because surgeons use knife and saw, and orthopedists construct and devise special appliances, are these specialists to be classed as mechanics or excluded from the class of medical men.* Yet plain as this may seem, the proposition has been vigorously disputed, and it has been stoutly maintained that one who cares for the teeth, call him dentist, odontologist, or stomatologist, is not a medical man following a surgical specialty, but is either a craftsman,† a trader,‡ or a member of a separate profession.§ And the reason is not far to seek. Ordinary dental operations require for their successful performance an unusual degree of manual dexterity and mechanical skill, to acquire which a considerable period of training is requisite. In our own century extraction of teeth was commonly performed by blacksmiths and barbers, while jewellers and ivory carvers made the artificial dental appliances. Later, dentists being noted rather for dexterity with tools than for scientific attainment, dentistry was associated chiefly with the mechanical work of extracting and repairing teeth and the manufacture of artificial substitutes

* "Is Dentistry a Specialty of Medicine?" *Medical Record*, vol. xxx., p. 642.

† State *ex rel.* Flickenger *v.* Fisher, 24 S. W., 167; s. c. 21 S. W., 446; *cf.* Maxon *v.* Perrot, 17 Mich., 332 ; Whitcomb *v.* Reed, 31 Miss., 567.

‡ Lee *v.* Griffin, 30 L. J. Q. B., 252 ; *cf.* French cases cited by Roger et Godon, "*Code de Chirurgien-Dentiste*," p. 88.

§ In some jurisdictions the practice of dentistry is defined by statute, *e.g.:*

In Minnesota a practitioner of dentistry is defined as one " who shall for a fee or salary or other reward, paid either to himself or for another person for operations or parts of operations of any kind, treat diseases or lesions of the human teeth or jaws, or correct malpositions thereof." Clearly this is a definition of a medical specialist.

In Dakota such a practitioner is defined as one " who shall perform upon the human teeth, or parts adjacent thereto, any operation or operations, such as are commonly known or designated as dental operations or operations in dental surgery, or who shall hold himself out by means of signs, cards, or advertisements as a dentist."

And see "A System of Legal Medicine," by Allan McLane Hamilton, and others, vol. i., p. 641.

for them.   To the ignorant or thoughtless a dentist is no more
a surgeon than is a truss-maker; they see only the mechanical
process, the art, and fail to note or apprehend that progress in
the science of dentistry, within very recent years, has been so
great and rapid as fully to entitle to rank among medical specialists its practitioners, who, within the memory of living man,
were, as Messrs. Godon and Roger point out,[*] as much the object of depreciation and ridicule as the physician or surgeon
of Molière's time.   Nor, indeed, do such persons realize how
recently it is in England that a surgeon has been regarded, by
those willing to intrust their lives to his care, as a person of
humble social position.[†]

As the physician has ceased to be called a " leech " and the
surgeon a " saw-bones," so has the dentist ceased to be described by cheap wits as a " tooth-carpenter "; and if the minds
of some persistently associate the dentist of to-day with the
old-time peripatetic extractor of teeth and maker of cumbrous
appliances, it is largely due to the unprofessional business
methods still adopted by certain persons, notably proprietors
of so-called " dental parlors," who, like the ancient barber-
surgeons of Henry VIII., "minding only their own lucres and
nothing the profit or ease of the diseased or patient," make
hideous displays to wayfarers; and by advertising cheap work,
snare poor patients, whom they commit to the hands of em-
ployees, too often ignorant, unskilful, and unlicensed.

It is because the due practice of operative dentistry requires
professional attainments of a high order—a general knowledge
of the human economy, and a very special knowledge of the
oral tract, its customary lesions, diseases, and abnormalities—as
well as manual dexterity, that laws prohibiting the ignorant
from such practice are distinctly legislation in the interest of

---

[*] " *Attaqué, calomnié, ridiculisé, comme le chirurgien ou le médecin au
temps de Molière, le dentiste a eu pendant une bonne partie du siècle, un
sort peu enviable.*"—"*Code de Chirurgien-Dentiste,*" par MM. Roger et
Godon, Paris, 1893.

[†] George Eliot, writing in our own time, makes one of her characters, Lady
Chettam, say: " Tell me about this new young surgeon, Mr. Lydgate. I am
told he is wonderfully clever. He certainly looks it—a fine brow, indeed!
Mr. Brooke says he is one of the Lydgates of Northumberland, really well
connected ; one does not expect it in a practitioner of that kind. For my
own part, I like a medical man more on the footing with the servants ; they
are often all the cleverer."—" Middlemarch."

the public health. The statute of New York recognizing this expressly exempts from its purview the "mechanical dentist," *i.e.*, the handicraftsman who works *in the laboratory upon inert matter.* Of this mechanic the operator, his employer, expects, it is true, excellence in his art; but the law exacts nothing. It is with the operator *whose work is upon the living organism* that the statute is concerned. As to him, the case is very different. No amount of manual skill alone can equip him to work intelligently or to the best results without anatomical, pathological, and therapeutical knowledge. To many it seems that the filling of a tooth is a purely mechanical operation, well performed if the cavity is "plugged" firmly and smoothly, and if no immediate pain results; that an extraction is a simple act, scarce worthy to be called an operation; and that the insertion of artificial teeth or dentures is a mere bit of handiwork entirely successful if mechanically accurate. Let a few examples suffice to illustrate how fallacious is this popular idea.

There came to a dentist of New York, who having been first graduated as a physician took up dentistry as a specialty, a patient seeking immediate relief from suffering due to the condition of his tongue which a surgeon had diagnosed as cancerous growth necessitating amputation. The dentist became satisfied that the condition was owing solely to traumatic lesions due to rough edges of the teeth. These latter he filed down, and applied slight local treatment to the inflamed organ. The patient was relieved, and by further treatment complete restoration of normal conditions resulted. A lady was sent from a Southern State to a leading surgeon of the same city with a request that he would operate to excise cancerous growth upon the tongue. He took the patient to a dentist, had certain teeth removed, and after local treatment sent her home entirely relieved, without the necessity of any operation. A neurologist sent to a dentist a patient who had for years suffered with acute facial neuralgia, to relieve which anodynes had been freely prescribed. An examination disclosed that the gums had grown over roots of a tooth that had been broken in the past by a clumsy effort at extraction. The local conditions being properly attended to, the pains no longer occurred; but the opium habit contracted under treatment remained.

When the Dental Act of France was debated prior to its

passage, the harm done by mere mechanicians in fitting artificial plates over diseased surfaces was fully brought out. A distinguished aurist of New York, now deceased, was wont to say that a large part of the diseases of the ear that he was called upon to relieve grew out of unwise dentistry; and Dr. Garretson, who beginning his medical career as a dentist, ended it as a distinguished oral surgeon, said as long ago as 1860, before the Pennsylvania Association of Dental Surgeons: "When, years back, before this association, I have spoken of anemia, chlorosis, and kindred conditions as the source of dental caries, I have been met with rebuke for travelling outside my profession. Let me now, gentlemen, add my mite to the experience of to-night by affirming that I believe I have saved more teeth by constitutional treatment than ever I have through manipulation." The same writer, in the preface to his fifth edition of "A System of Oral Surgery," written in 1890, says: "Oral surgery, twenty years back, was without so much as a name. To-day, oral surgery as a specialty in medicine is not surpassed, as to its range and as to requirements looked for on the part of its practitioners, by any department of the healing art. . . . Where medical knowledge is lacking, dentistry is of little use to a community." To go further into this matter here, even if the lay writer were, as he is not, competent to treat the question from the technical standpoint of oral surgery, would transgress the prescribed limits of this discussion. Enough has certainly been said to show that those laymen who see in the dentist only a craftsman, and those dentists who aim to be nothing more than craftsmen, have a very superficial and poor idea of what dentistry is, as practised by its leading men, and what it should be if patients are to receive adequate treatment at the hands of dental practitioners.

The Pharmacist as a Medical Man.

Just as the dentist has been popularly regarded as a mere mechanic to whom special medical knowledge was unnecessary, so the pharmacist has been considered as nothing more than a tradesman, although in fact he is constantly practising medicine, or, as the phrase is, "counter-prescribing." It has been already pointed out how, through public toleration of their irregular practice in England, apothecaries—who were formerly there, as they still are with us, mere dispensers of drugs —came eventually to be general medical practitioners; the titles "chemist," "chemist and druggist," and "pharmaceutical chemist" coming into use instead of the older name.

That it may be desirable for an apothecary, pharmacist, or druggist to have some medical knowledge would appear from the fact, or alleged fact, that compounders of prescriptions have been known to save life either by calling attention to grave mistakes, or, where they have feared to wound *amour propre* and lose custom, by quietly correcting errors. On the other hand, it is forcibly argued that the medical education of a pharmacist, short of what is required for the physician's degree, is a direct incentive to irregular practice. There is no space here to review that discussion; nor is there any doubt that the dispensing pharmacist or druggist is in some degree a medical man who should be educated in his business.

Differentiations of Medical Men.

The questions obviously arising out of the regulation of general medical, dental, and pharmaceutical practice by separate laws make it apparent that hopeless confusion would result if the practice of every medical specialty were separately regulated. The fact that laryngologists, gynecologists, oculists, and other specialists are equipped for practice by the same general course of medical study and training, and usually drift into special from general work, operates to create *esprit du corps*, to prevent friction among them, and to obviate efforts by one of them to prohibit encroachment by others upon his field. But the pharmacist who is not licensed to practise medicine has been frequently punished for his violation of law in prescribing a remedy over his counter; and although general systemic treatment of his patient by a dentist, unlicensed to practise general medicine, has not yet been made a ground of prosecution under medical laws, such prosecutions have been suggested; and *vice versa*, it has been argued that physicians are liable to prosecution who treat the teeth without a dental license. While a license to practise medicine would be a complete protection to the prescribing druggist, thorough medi-

cal education is not likely to be required or sought by those intending to engage in that business which, strictly speaking, does
not imply personal relations with the patients. But practice of
dentistry does involve of necessity the exercise of medical and
surgical knowledge, and the relation of operator and patient;
therefore the possession by dentists of the medical degree
would seem very desirable, and the drift is to that requirement.
Already many physicians with surgical and mechanical apti-
tude have limited their practice to treatment of the oral cavity,
and these it has been proposed to distinguish as stomatologists,
leaving the name dentist to designate those who do only mechanical work. But it seems unnecessary to express an opinion here on this debated nomenclature.

It is to be hoped—perhaps more hoped than expected—that
a new generation will find the jarring medical sects united in
a common accord. A long step in this direction was taken in
New York, when the Act of 1887 codifying the penal features
of the medical law was passed. Thitherto every attempt to
secure legislation made by regular practitioners had been stren-
uously opposed by homœopaths and eclectics, as well as by the
army of Christian scientists, clairvoyants, magnetists, mind
curers, faith curers, truss-makers, and all those wishing to engage in the business of healing the sick without training or
study. But when convinced that the proposed law was not a
covert attack upon their medical theories, the homœopaths
earnestly favored it and materially helped its passage; while
the eclectics withheld or modified their usual opposition. The
enactment of that law paved the way for the existing system
of medical license whereunder three examining boards exist,
and candidates having passed uniform examinations in those
branches of medical science in which there is no schism, elect
the system of therapeutics in which they will be examined. If
it be true, as said, that the differences between the enlightened
practitioners of the various schools are already nominal rather
than real, it may not be oversanguine to expect, with the
growth of accurate knowledge, an obliteration of the schools
and a unification of the profession. In proportion as practice
is founded upon certain and scientifically acquired knowledge, upon carefully observed facts rather than fanciful theo-
rizing, the differences of medical men tend to disappear, or to
become differences of opinion in particular cases rather than

on general principles; and in this fact lies the hope of future medical harmony.

To this end the enforcement of medical legislation is believed by those who favor it to conduce.

The Need of Examining Boards Illustrated.

An amusing and instructive volume might be made up from answers of candidates for medical and dental licenses before the examining boards of the several States. We are so habituated in the ordinary business of life to accepting men at their own valuation, to attaching undue importance to diplomas and school certificates, that many fail to appreciate the value of the system that interposes an impartial State examining board between the people and the graduates of medical colleges desirous of practising medicine upon the strength of their diplomas alone. A wall is only as strong as its weakest, a fence no higher than its lowest, part. Wherever the so-called diploma standard of qualification exists, the poorest diploma recognized sets that standard. Only a few years ago throughout the country the fraudulent diplomas of Buchanan and others of his kidney afforded, as they still afford in some localities, the standard of licenses.

When in New York any one was allowed to practise medicine who held the diploma of a chartered medical school, the profession was invaded and the public imposed upon by illiterate and incompetent practitioners holding so-called diplomas, obtained after mere formal attendance at lectures or by downright purchase *in absentia*. " Colleges " were organized as matter of business. Even the best institutions were over-lenient from an ill-founded fear of diminishing the number of students, and the consequent revenues. To-day in that State a diploma from the best medical school—from Harvard, or the College of Physicians and Surgeons in New York itself—will not operate as a license to practise, but its holder must submit to examination before a State board. The same is true of diplomas from dental colleges. The result of establishing these State boards has been, it is believed, good as a rule; but the best results are obtained where, as in New York, the possession of a diploma confers no right to practise, but is

2

only a necessary prerequisite to the privilege of going up for examination before the State board of examiners.

A few examples of answers to questions from examination papers will show that a student may acquire a diploma from colleges of a certain sort without acquiring that knowledge desirable in one who ministers to man's physical infirmities. These examples, it should be said, while *bona fide*, are not chosen from the examination papers of any one State.

The following have been taken from papers of candidates for license to practise medicine:

Q. What are your views as to the efficacy of vaccination?

A. I don't believe into it.*

Q. What is the length of the intestines?

A. (This question has been variously answered by candidates with estimates varying from three feet to three hundred yards.)

Q. How many bones are there in the human body?

A. Very many indeed, the principal ones however are the bones of the head and the pelvis. The former are thin the latter thick. All other bones are long.

Q. Give the chemical formula of sulfuric acid.

A. Not correctly spelled. Should be sulphuric acid—the wrong spelling is probably to make it a catch question,—the missing "ph" in the spelling being the formula of the acid.†

Q. What is the composition of atmospheric air?

A. Carbon, hydrogen, Smoke and various germs of disease in epidemic seasons.

Q. The head of the child in the superior strait—forceps frequently applied but slip off on traction, pain lessening, mother growing weaker—what is your duty?

A. Send for the man who is to mark these answer papers if he will but reveal his identity.

Q. Describe the *lobus Spigelii.*‡

A. A plant indigenous to South America of which the leaves alone are used. It is a stomachic—dose of the tincture 30 drops.

---

* The question itself might have been better framed. Doubtless the candidate fully expressed "his views."

† The spelling seems to have been a concession—and a mistaken one—to the examiners' theory of phonetics. The symbol asked for is H_2SO_4.

‡ One lobe of the liver. The botanic genus Spigelia is named after Van der Spiegel, and may have been in the candidate's mind.

Q. What is understood by extra-uterine pregnancy?

A. Pregnancy *without* the uterus as for instance in the Eustachian tube.*

The following questions and answers are from papers of candidates for license to practise dentistry:

Q. What is the difference between Materia Medica and Therapeutics?

A. Materia Medica treats origin and physical properties, while Therapeutics treats of drudgon the system.

Q. What is the use of an anæsthetic?

A. To perform a painful operation it is necessary but some patitients are susepitable to anæsthetics. these patitients are dibetic patitient, consumption, ænemic patitient. Alcohol patitient that loss a quantity of blood this patitient it is necessary to build before use of anesthetics—or on a full stomach.

Q. What are physiological effects of sulphuric ether while inhaled?

A. It produces semiplastic condition of nerus cell, hence complete anæsthesia first excite muscular contraction increases flow of saliva, opeon of eperglotis and reflex action of swoling, feeling of sufication and other inconveniences.

Q. What are the effects of chloroform when inhaled?

A. Chloroform produces Death by perichysizing Heart. First increases inspiratiin three or four minutes not as long as ether but more dangerous. Very short notice patitient pass away without notice. Same physiological as ether only it effect heart while ether only effect resp.

Q. What is the difference between an abscess and an ulcer?

A. Abscess contains pus and an ulcer does not.

Q. What is the cause of the variation of color in decay?

A. Sometimes chewing tobacco sometimes food get in cavity and form sort of white decay.

Q. Give treatment of cocaine poisoning.

A. Avoide the administration.

Q. When is the use of an anæsthetic contraindicated?

---

* This candidate seems to have had the same theory as Agnes in Molière's *"L'Ecole des Femmes,"* acte i., scène 1 :

    "Elle étoit fort en peine, et me vint demander,
    Avec une innocence à nulle autre pareille,
    Si les enfants qu'on fait se faisoient par l'oreille."

A. In case of a painful operation when the patient is capable of taking such.

Q. What are the fluids of the mouth?

A. Spit.

Q. How would you treat a fracture of the inferior maxillary?

A. Treat with Carbolic Acid and lime water, keep the parts cool.

Q. Give the treatment of wounds of the tongue.

A. Treatment of wounds of the tongue are three. Continuity, Conditunity, Caseuify.

Q. Define plastic surgery. Describe the methods that may be employed in plastic surgery.

To this question the three answers following were given:

(1) Plastic surgery is used when you use plaster on the surface instead of sowing up a wound, and is also used to assist to hold a wound that has been sowed up so that it won't pull out. Use as counter irretants, etc.

(2) Staphylosoplasty would be a case of a plastic operation. The uniting of the parts together without the use of a surgical operation. For example in a cleft palate plastic operations are often times successful, by drawing parts together and keeping same in such a way by use of, in this case, plaster of Paris, when parts held in such way will in time unite.

(3) Plastic surgery may apply to M.D. or D.D.S. In fractures of bones the fractures may be reduced and set in plaster of paris. For the M.D. The plastic fillings in the teeth, example, mixing H_3 p.O_4 and oxide of xinz and is called an oxphosefate filling. This is plastic work.

The Methods of Enforcing Medical Laws.

It remains, finally, to say a word as to the manner in which medical laws are enforced.

The argument that an unenforced law is worse than useless, is well known. It is by enforcement that a statute becomes familiar in a general way to the public, which by a most violent legal presumption is supposed to know law often unknown either to court or counsel. It is through enforcement that the law acts as a schoolmaster. Unenforced yet unrepealed, a penal statute, if its existence be generally known, breeds con-

tempt for law, or if its provisions have fallen into forgetful-
ness, proves a snare to the unwary.   There is an unfortunately
increasing tendency, of late years, toward regulating by statute
all employments, customs, and ordinary acts of men.   This is
due in part to the plague of annual legislatures.   No better
examples of eccentric legislation can be found than two laws
on the New York statute-book.   One of them—which has never
been enforced in a single instance, so far as the writer knows—
makes liable to fine and imprisonment any person, even a child,
who feeds an English sparrow, the *passer domesticus.*   The
other makes it a misdemeanor for a Brooklyn barber to shave a
customer on Sunday, although at the same time Figaro in New
York may lawfully render that service; in other words, makes
an act of cleanliness and comfort lawful at one end of Brooklyn Bridge, but criminal at the other.*   Not only occupations
obviously affecting to a marked degree public morals and
health, such as the sale of alcoholic stimulants and the practice of medicine, but also such pursuits as bookkeeping and
horse-shoeing, have been taken into legislative care.   It is perfectly plain that laws of this kind cannot and should not be
systematically administered by the municipal police, as some
enthusiasts vigorously contend.   The true function of the uniformed police force is to protect life and property, to preserve
order and decency in public places, and to execute warrants
issued by police magistrates.   Of its own initiative that force
should ferret out crimes of violence that have escaped observa-
tion; but of its own initiative it should not engage systematically
in detecting the violation of these laws merely regulative of occupations and customary acts or morals; to do so would take the
officers from their proper duties, and, worst of all, would tre-
mendously increase the temptation to blackmail that is now, as
it has always been, the besetting sin of men hired to preserve
order.   Here again we confront a large topic that cannot in
this place be fully dealt with.   But it will be difficult for any
one becoming familiar with the question to resist the conclusion that the uniformed police force should not customarily
engage in the work of detecting stealthy breaches of laws relating to what are known, for want of a better classification, as
mala prohibita in contrast with *mala in se,* and in degree amounting only to misdemeanors.   The proposition that the police

* People *v.* Havnor, 149 N. Y., 195.

should systematically procure evidence that persons have been guilty of unlawfully tossing crumbs to sparrows, totting up accounts, or even practising medicine, needs only to be stated to demonstrate its intrinsic absurdity.

In fact, medical laws are customarily enforced, if at all, by organizations, to whose members they are matters of special interest, such as medical, dental, and pharmaceutical societies, or boards, or colleges. Some of these bodies, like the State Dental Society of New York, are expressly authorized by statute to lay informations before magistrates to aid in prosecutions, and to receive wholly or in part the fines imposed in cases prosecuted by them. Others, like the incorporated County Medical Societies of New York, are authorized to receive the fines and by implication to assist in the prosecution. In their work such societies employ agents to examine reported cases and ascertain by investigation who are practising without the required license and registration.

Obviously these agents are exposed on the one hand to the temptation to exact toll from the suspected, *i.e.*, to become themselves a source of license, and on the other to false accusation by those upon whom they keep watch. Herein is the strongest argument against these laws.

Again, the temptation to "make a record," as the phrase is, may lead zealous agents, or even the officer or attorney charged with the conduct of such a society's prosecutions, to overlook the true purpose of the law, and in zeal for his own interest to forget the duty that is owing to the accused by prosecutors. Over-zealous and unfair prosecutions, resting upon no better evidence than that of hired detectives, are quite certain in the long run to work the repeal of an ill-administered law. That statutes of the sort referred to cannot be enforced systematically without the employment of detective agents, seems demonstrated by experience, which equally demonstrates the advisability of corroborating the testimony of those agents by that of actual patients, and of supervising their acts by persons having it always in view that the purpose of the law is the prevention of the evil, and not the personal advantage of any one, whether the prosecuting society, its counsel, or agent, and that the chief good to be hoped for from the statute's enforcement is its educational and deterrent effect.

Besides securing the systematic enforcement of the law under careful supervision, the intervention of these societies has the further advantage that it affords to persons falsely accused careful investigation of the charge, and adequate redress by an action of false arrest or malicious prosecution, which, if prosecuted against a police officer, public detective, or agent of such a society, would yield at best a barren victory, but if prosecuted against the incorporated society is likely to afford full reparation to any one wronged by an untruthful accusation, whether made with actual malicious intent or out of inexcusable carelessness. Moreover, the very consciousness that such actions are possible,—and they have been not infrequently brought,— tends to make the officers of prosecuting societies more careful, and thus affords practitioners adequate protection against false accusations.

As has been suggested elsewhere,* the conviction of the ordinary unlicensed practitioner is of value chiefly in that its public announcement by the press serves the double purpose of keeping the public reminded that charlatanism is rife and in deterring the ignorant from attempting to assume the work of the learned. There are also special cases which illustrate more strongly than do the average, the benefit that may accrue to the public generally from the enforcement of the laws under consideration by the societies referred to.

In February, 1893, Alfred Booth, styling himself M.D. and Ph.D., opened an office, *i.e.*, took a room in a little hotel in Tenth Street, in New York city, where he entered upon the sale of diplomas of the Excelsior Medical College of Massachusetts. His price for a degree of Doctor of Medicine was $50, and for an additional $25 he conferred also the degree of Ph.D. His proceedings having been brought to the knowledge of the County Medical Society by the New York *Herald*, he was arrested and sentenced to a term of six months in the penitentiary, the sentence being light in consideration of the defendant's plea of guilty and his advanced age of seventy years. In the following July, Walter May Rew, a man of considerable ability, engaged in similar business, information of which was given by the same newspaper, and in the following October he, too, was sentenced to a term of imprisonment upon

* "How Far can Legislation Aid in Maintaining a Proper Standard of Medical Education?" A paper read before the American Social Science Association, at Saratoga, September 5, 1888.

his plea of guilty. Both of these men cynically offered to give, for trifling sums, to absolutely ignorant persons, certificates that would lead the unsuspecting to suppose the holders to be well-equipped physicians. One of these men, when asked by the person to whom he sold a " diploma " what the latter should do about a death certificate in case a patient should die, replied in writing: " When I say that the diagnoses of forty per cent. of death certificates are guesses, hazarded on insufficient data, and are very often erroneous, you need not be much afraid to hazard a guess also."

Equally striking instances may be found in the prosecutions under the Dental Law. In 1895, Jesse Gagnon engaged with his brother George in advertising dental business in New York city, the two conducting the so-called New York Dental Parlors and the New System Dental Parlors. In December of that year Jesse was arrested upon the charge of practising under the false name of Thomas E. Jackson, a graduate of the Western Dental College of Kansas City. Inquiry at that college was answered by a statement that the Thomas E. Jackson there graduated had been killed, as the authorities were informed, in Illinois, and had written a short time before his death to ask for a copy of his diploma, alleging that the original was lost. Further inquiry by the State Society disclosed that Gagnon had been proceeded against in other States for violation of dental laws. A person in his employ at the time of arrest made affidavit that he had been instructed by defendant to assume falsely the title of Doctor and a name not his own, and had been further advised that his business would be to get as much money as possible from patients. He was further prepared to testify that upon taking employment he was told that the work done cheaply was ill done, and would necessitate the return of the patient for further treatment. After delaying the prosecution for two years by demurrer and dilatory procedure, the defendant was at last arraigned for trial, pleaded guilty to the offence charged, and paid a fine of $500, the highest that could be imposed under the statute.

Further citation of examples would seem scarcely necessary to justify legislation to protect the public against such misdoing.

Notes of American Legal Decisions

AFFECTING MEDICAL PRACTITIONERS AND THE PUBLIC HEALTH.

THE following cases, revised to date of going to press, deal for the most part with topics touched upon in the article entitled "Of Certain Legal Relations of Physicians and Surgeons to Their Patients and to One Another," in "A System of Legal Medicine," by Allan McLane Hamilton and others (E. B. Treat & Co., New York, 1894–99). References have been made, therefore, to that work, in order that those having copies of it might annotate them, and those wishing to investigate the principles involved in the following cases might be furnished with anterior authorities. The large number of decisions cited—one hundred and thirty-five in number—renders it impossible, within the allotted space, to do more, as a rule, than indicate their salient points; but cases involving matter of special interest have been more fully stated. Under the modern system of American reporting, any one desiring a full report of a case can, by citing the reference, procure a copy of the Reporter containing it, at an average cost of twenty-five cents, from the West Publishing Company, of St. Paul, Minn.

The abbreviations A., Pac., N.E., N.W., S.E., and S.W., indicate the Atlantic, Pacific, Northeastern, Northwestern, Southeastern and Southwestern Reporters; N.Y.S., App. Div., and Misc., indicate respectively New York Supplement, Appellate Division, and Miscellaneous Reports; N.Y.L.J., New York Law Journal; L.J.R., Q.B.Div.—Law Journal Reporter, Queen's Bench Division. Other abbreviations of State and English Reports are obvious.

Pages in Hamilton refer to the first volume, unless the second is specified.

W. A. PURRINGTON,

59 WALL STREET, January 16, 1899.

I. Statutory Regulation of Medical Practice.

Who Is a Physician—Evidence (Ham., p. 602). HOLDING
OUT.—A. went to B., a druggist, believing him to be a doctor
also, to have an injured finger treated. B. treated the finger
wrongly for ten days, necessitating amputation. A. brought an
action to recover damages for malpractice.

Held, that if B. "treated, operated on, or prescribed for any
physical ailment," he was practising medicine within the Illinois statute; that if he held himself out to A. as a doctor, and
A. believed him to be such, he was liable for failing to exercise the skill and care of a doctor; and whether the facts of
those premises were true, was for the jury to say.

Matthei *v.* Wooley, 69 Ill. App., 654.

"Christian Scientists."—In Rhode Island, A., who undertook for a money consideration to cure malaria, grippe, and
whatever other diseases persons who came to him "imagined
they had," was indicted for practising medicine unlawfully.
Upon the testimony it appeared that he gave those who came
to him pamphlets on Christian Science and apparently engaged
in silent prayer, but gave no drugs or medicines, used no surgical instruments, and made neither examination nor diagnosis. He testified that he did not attempt to cure disease, that
he knew nothing of medicine or surgery, and that his only
method was "prayer and effort to encourage hopefulness for
all who come to him in public or private, and whatever diseases they imagine they have."

Held, that, under the statute of that State, A. was not practising medicine; that if Christian Science be practice of medicine, it is a school, and entitled to recognition by the State
board under the laws which forbid discrimination against
medical schools, since to prescribe requirements with which a
particular school could not comply would be not to discrimi-
nate only, but to prohibit.

State *v.* Mylod, 40 Atl., 753.

(Cf. State *v.* Buswell, 40 Neb., 158, A.D. 1894, where it was
held, on the contrary, that a Christian Scientist using the
above methods only was practising medicine within the meaning of the Nebraska statute. See sub-title "Manslaughter,"
below, under main title "Miscellaneous." And, as to dis-

crimination against schools, see that sub-title under "Constitutionality of Laws," below, in this division.)

In an unreported Maryland case, Wright, J., held that no fees could be recovered for faith-cure treatment.

Doty *v.* Winters, Oct. 27, 1897.

A., charged with unlawfully practising medicine and surgery, admitted that he was not a licensed or registered physician. It appeared that he acted in conjunction with one Dr. B., a duly registered physician, and another, Dr. C., not shown to be registered; that the three operated jointly, and divided the remuneration equally. A. offered evidence to show that he operated and administered remedies under B.'s directions. The prosecution offered evidence to show that he also acted without B.'s instructions in B.'s absence. The trial court charged that if A. did not practise on his own account, but acted under B.'s direction, the jury should find him not guilty.

Held, on appeal, that this was error; that under the Nebraska statute any person, not expressly exempted from its operation, who "operates on, professes to heal or prescribe for or otherwise treat any physical or mental ailment of another," is practising medicine, whether he acts on his own account or under the direction of a registered practitioner, and that whether he professes himself to be a legal and competent practitioner or not makes no difference.

State *v.* Paul, 76 N.W., 861.

Dentistry.—Practice is established by showing that the accused leased and occupied rooms for the avowed purpose of there practising, did dental work there for three or more persons, filled teeth, and worked at the bench.

Ferner *v.* State, 51 N.E., 360 (Ind.).

"Osteopathy."—A. engaged in "the profession of osteopathy," received and visited patients, advertised his system and skill, professed ability to understand and treat human ailments intelligently and successfully, including fevers, cerebro-spinal meningitis, catarrh, diphtheria, croup, pneumonia, and other diseases. His treatment consisted wholly of rubbing and manipulating afflicted parts and flexing the limbs.

Held, that he practised medicine within the definition of the Illinois statute; that by professing to diagnose diseases and give discriminating treatment, he differed from masseurs and those giving Turkish baths; that Smith *v.* Lane did not apply

—the New York statute differing from that of Illinois, and the facts of the cases being different.

> Eastman *v.* People ex rel. St. Bd. of Health, 71 Ill., App., 236.

In Ohio, on the contrary, it was held that an "osteopath" is not a practitioner of medicine within the statute.

> Eastman *v.* State, 6 Ohio Dec., 296 (Jan., 1897).

Constitutionality of Laws (Ham., p. 596).—The principle involved was fully discussed in Dent *v.* W. Va., 129 U. S., 114 (1889), and other cases cited in Hamilton.

EX POST FACTO LAWS.—VESTED RIGHTS.—A., convicted in New York of a felony in 1877, served a term of imprisonment. Long after the expiration of his term, a statute was enacted in that State, making guilty of misdemeanor any person "who after conviction of a felony shall attempt to practise medicine." Under this statute, A. was indicted, for that having been so convicted, he, thereafter, practised medicine unlawfully by treating and prescribing for one H. contrary to the statute. Upon his admission of said conviction and subsequent practice of medicine, A. was found guilty of unlawfully practising contrary to the statute. Apparently the record did not show that he was ever licensed as a physician. On appeal, the Appellate Division, admitting the constitutionality of said provision of the law in its application *in futuro*, reversed the conviction upon the ground that said statute, in depriving A. of his right to practise on account of a felony committed before its enactment, imposed an additional penalty for that crime, and was *ex post facto*. The Court of Appeals reversed the Appellate Division, apparently on the ground that, as it nowhere appeared in the record that A. ever had a right to practise medicine, there was no proof that he was deprived of any right or ever had any right to so practise, wherefore such practice on his part was misdemeanor, without regard to whether or not he had committed the felony and been punished therefor. The Supreme Court of the United States, by a divided bench, disregarding the defect of the record, affirmed the validity of the law in its operation upon persons convicted of felonies prior to its enactment—holding said provision to be not a new punishment, but a regulation dependent on character of which such a conviction was evidence.

> People *v.* Hawker, 14 App. Div., 188 ; S. C., 152 ; N. Y.,

234. Hawker *v.* People of New York, 170; U. S., 189; 18 Sup. Ct. R., 573. See *Medical Record* of July 24, 1897, vol. lii., p. 114.

The Ohio statute containing a similar provision was held to be prospective and constitutional.

France *v.* State, 57 Ohio St., 1; 47 N.E., 1,041 (Oct. 26, 1897).

A., being licensed to practise in Indiana at the time the law of 1897 took effect, was refused a license by the board created under that law, upon the ground that his previous license had been procured fraudulently. Upon his application for a writ of mandamus, directing the board to issue to him a license—

Held, that the law of 1897, forbidding medical practice without license, making existing licenses revocable upon failure of their holders to comply with the law's provisions, and permitting the licensing board to refuse its certificates to felons or persons grossly immoral or unfit for a physician's duties by reason of addiction to drugs or liquors, was valid, and not an unconstitutional interference with vested rights.

State *v.* Webster, 150 Ind., 607; 50 N.E., 750.

See also

State *v.* Morrill, 7 Ohio Dec., 52. Commonwealth *v.* Wilson, 19 Pa. Co. Ct. R., 521 (Aug., 1897). Re Roe Chung, 49 Pac., 952 (New Mexico, August, 1897).

DENTAL LAWS (Ham., p. 643).—The Pennsylvania statute forbidding practice of dentistry except in compliance with its terms, does not abridge the privileges and immunities of citizens unconstitutionally.

Commonwealth *v.* Gibson, 7 Pa. Dist. R., 386.

So held also in Indiana.

Ferner *v.* State, 51 N.E., 360 (*supra*).

Discrimination against Medical Schools.—In Texas, A. sued B. to recover fees for medical services. B. defended on the ground, among other things, that A. was not entitled to practise, not having a certificate from any board of medical examiners of the State. It was undisputed that A. held a diploma of the Eclectic Medical Institute of Cincinnati, duly chartered and accredited in Ohio, and had recorded it as required by law in the district clerk's office; but that he had no certificate from any Texas board. The Constitution of Texas prescribes that the legislature may establish by law qualifications for practitioners of medicine, providing, however, that "no preference shall ever be given by law to any school of medicine." The qualification prescribed by the statute is a certificate by a board of examiners composed of physicians, "graduates of some medical college recognized by the American Medical Association." It was undisputed evidence that said Association recognized only "allopaths" or "regulars," so-called, but not eclectics, and the plaintiff contended that the statute was unconstitutional.

Held, that the mere fact that the board was directed to be so composed did not necessarily prefer the regular school and so render the statute unconstitutional, and that it would not be presumed that the board in its examinations would violate the law. Judgment for defendant was therefore affirmed.

Dowdell *v.* McBride, 45 S.W., 397.

EXEMPTIONS OF CONSULTANTS FROM OTHER STATES AND OTHERS.—The Ohio statute forbidding physicians of other States from practising in Ohio, except as consultants, is not unconstitutional as abridging the privileges and immunities of citizens of the United States or of the several States.

France *v.* State, 57 Ohio St., 1 (*supra*).

Nor does that of North Carolina, which exempts from its operation those practising in the State at the time of its enactment, grant exclusive privileges and emoluments, or create monopolies and perpetuities in violation of the constitution.

State *v.* Call, 28 S.E., 517.

So, also, a statute is valid, although it exempt from its provisions medical officers of the United States, of hospital staffs, etc. (Ham., p. 604).

Commonwealth *v.* Wilson, 19 Pa. Co. Ct. R., 521 (*supra*).

Application of Licensing Laws.—DENTAL.—The Pennsylvania act does not apply to those practising in the State at the time of its enactment.

Commonwealth *v.* Gibson (*supra*).

The Maryland statute's exemption from its purview of those holding certificates obtained prior to its enactment, refers only to certificates issued in Maryland, not to those given in other States.

Knowles *v.* State, 39 Atl., 619.

Pharmaceutical.—The New York public health law exempts from the category of pharmacists, medical practitioners not proprietors of stores for retailing drugs.

Held, not to prevent one physician from compounding another's prescription, notwithstanding that pharmacy is defined to be, among other things, the compounding of prescriptions to be used with medicines.

Held, also, that a physician does not come within the scope of the law unless engaged in the business of pharmacy.

Suffolk Co. *v.* Shaw, 21 App. Div., 146.

Registration (Ham., p. 600).—A physician registered prior to March 1, 1894, in one county of Pennsylvania, under the Act of June 8, 1881, may still, after the passage of the Act of May 18, 1893, practise in any county of the State.

Commonwealth *v.* Townley, 7 Pa. Dist. R., 413.

Transient Offices.—A., renting an office by the year and keeping regular office hours thrice weekly, is not indictable under the Pennsylvania statute for keeping a transient office.

Commonwealth *v.* Townley (*supra*).

Powers of Examining and Licensing Boards (Ham., pp. 598, 599).

An Oregon State board, having power to license without examination holders of medical diplomas, refused to license A. It was succeeded by a new board, with power to license only after examination.

Held, that the new board could not review its predecessor's action, and license A. without examination.

Miller *v.* Board of Med. Examiners, 52 Pac., 763.

In Oklahoma, the superintendent of public health, and not the board of health, is the proper authority to license physicians.

Weeden *v.* Arnold, 49 Pac., 915 (July, 1897).

To practise lawfully in Texas, one must comply with the provisions of the statute creating examining boards, although it omits a provision contained in the previous statute, forbidding any one to practise except those who had complied with the law.

Dowdell *v.* McBride, 45 S.W., 397.

A., charged with unlawful practice in Ohio, cannot show that the examining board's refusal of a certificate was improper; nor can the courts review the action of the board in exercising its discretion to grant or refuse certificates of a right to practise.

Kowenstrot *v.* State, 8 Ohio Dec., 119; 15 Ohio Cir., 73.
(This case is given upon the authority of the American Digest; the report itself not being accessible.)

In Oregon, an appeal lies from the decision of the examining board to the Circuit Court, whose judgment may in turn be appealed from by the board.

The State is a proper party to a proceeding to revoke licenses for unprofessional conduct which is quasi-criminal in character; and it is sufficient to serve notice of appeal upon the State without serving the relators or the board.

The provision requiring the board to license persons presenting certificates of registration within ninety days from the passage of the Amendatory Act of 1891, is mandatory.

State *v.* Estes, 52 Pac., 571.

The Iowa statute authorizes the State board of medical examiners to revoke medical licenses, among other causes, "for palpable evidence of incompetency." Upon a petition purporting to be signed by five physicians, accompanied by a certified transcript of proceedings before a coroner in the case of B., deceased, and asking that A.'s certificate be revoked for incompetency therein appearing, the board furnished A. with a copy of the charges against him, and notified him to appear and answer them. Upon his failure so to do, the board upon such documentary evidence revoked his certificate.

Held, that the board had jurisdiction and its acts could not be reviewed on certiorari. At most, it acted upon evidence that might have been excluded if objected to.

Traer *v.* State Board of Med. Exam., 76 N.W., 833.

Pleading and Procedure.

In Ohio, an indictment is defective if it only charge that the accused has practised without a certificate, but fail (1) to allege that he has omitted to do those acts entitling him to its issuance, or (2) to indicate to what class of persons described in the statute he belongs.

State *v.* Morrill, 7 Ohio Dec., 52.

The Rhode Island statute forbidding unlicensed practice of

medicine provides a fine only in cases where the practice is for compensation.

Held, that to make out a violation of the statute the accused must be shown to have received reward for his practice (*cf.* Ham., p. 603).

State *v.* Pirlot, 38 Atl., 656.

But it has been held that intent to receive fees is equivalent to actual receipt of them.

State *v.* Hale, 15 Mo., 606 (cited in Ham., p. 603).

In New York, under the statute regulating the practice of veterinary surgery—

Held, that if the complaint, in an action for a penalty, only allege practice at a certain time and place in violation of the statute, it is defective as stating a mere legal conclusion.

Held, also, that it should negative the exemptions of the enacting clause.

Steuben Co. *v.* Wood, 24 App. Div., 442; 48 N.Y.S., 471.

In Ohio and North Carolina, the exemptions, not being in the enacting clause, need not be negatived.

Kowenstrot *v.* State, 15 Ohio Cir. Ct. R., 73. Hale *v.* State, 51 N.E., 154. State *v.* Call, 28 S.E., 517.

In North Carolina, an indictment failing to allege that the accused had not obtained a certificate or registered, is defective. But it need not allege that the unlawful practice charged was for fee or reward, although a special verdict must find that fact; nor need it negative the exemptions of the statute.

State *v.* Call, 28 S.E., 517 (*supra*).

Imprisonment for Non-Payment of Fines.

The act of New Mexico, providing that defendant adjudged in an action of debt to pay a forfeiture for unlawfully practising medicine may be imprisoned on default in payment, is valid.

Re Roe Chung, 49 Pac., 952 (*supra*).

II. Fees—Compensation (Ham., 604).

License Presumed in Civil Action.—If A., practising as a physician, attend and treat B. in that capacity, his authority so to practise will be presumed in an action brought to recover

3

his fees. If he be not licensed (or registered), the burden of proving that fact is upon B. In criminal cases the rule is otherwise.

Lacy *v.* Kossuth County (Iowa), 75 N.W., 689.

Compensation for Attending County Poor AT REQUEST OF OFFICIALS.—(See below "Public Health," sub-title "Compensation.")

Value of Services—EVIDENCE OF.—If a physician renders professional services without special contract as to the amount of remuneration, and brings an action to recover their value, a fellow physician may testify whether the bill is reasonable or not.

Ward *v.* Ohio River & C. R.R. Co., 30 S.E., 594.

(It may be noted that this action was against a corporation, and therefore not for services rendered to defendant as a patient. The nature of the services does not appear, and the question of privilege was not raised. Where, however, a physician sues a patient to recover the value of services, and calls another physician to testify to their nature, the latter's testimony will be inadmissible if it violates the statutory privilege of the patient and is objected to.)

See McGillicuddy *v.* Farmers' Loan and Trust Co., *infra*, under "Evidence," sub-title "Privilege of Professional Communications."

Valueless Services—PHYSICIAN'S FAILURE TO INFORM PATIENT OF HIS HOPELESS CONDITION IS A DEFENCE.—A., a specialist in diseases of the nose, throat, and ear, sued B. to recover $160 fees. B. testified that, having had nasal catarrh for ten years, he submitted to A.'s treatment for some months, paid $122, and, experiencing no relief, discontinued it for a year; thereafter he returned to A., saying he had no money to throw away, but was willing to pay well if he could be cured. A. said, "I can't tell you now," but gave sixty-five treatments, saying each time, "Your nose is getting along beautifully, beautifully." B. still complaining, A. said he was going to New York and would consult Dr. C. in the case. During A.'s absence, his father, also a physician, gave some treatment, and said that his son had always considered the case incurable. On A.'s return, B said: "I can't afford to take your treatment unless you can cure me." A. replied: "If you will come back now I can cure you. I can perform an operation in your head.

I have had a talk with Dr. C. about this; he says I can cure you." A. testified that he had treated the case with "sprays and trichloricetic acid so as to allow a drainage from above as much as possible," and that was the best treatment anybody knew; that on his return he told B. that he did not think his case would improve unless he submitted to an operation to open the frontal sinus, which was a *dernier ressort*, practised only in extreme cases, and sometimes successful; he could not say that it would have cured B., who testified that he had improved in general and local condition since discontinuing A.'s treatment. On appeal from a judgment for plaintiff on a verdict—

Held, granting a new trial, that it was A.'s duty to act in utmost good faith toward B.; that, while a physician is held only to reasonable skill and knowledge and is not a guarantor, the law will not countenance quackery; and if A. should have seasonably discovered in the exercise of such skill that B.'s case would not yield to the usual treatment, or probably would not be benefited by it, and failed so to advise B., he was guilty of negligence, and the trial court erred in not so charging the jury whose function it was to decide whether A. had not discovered before his trip to New York that his treatment was abortive.

Held, also, that if A.'s services and treatment were worthless and ineffective to work a cure, there could be no recovery of compensation; and that the jury should have been charged that if B.'s failure to reap benefit was due to A.'s lack of, or failure to exercise, ordinary knowledge, skill, and care, there could be no recovery.

Logan *v*. Field, 75 Mo. App. R., 594.

Autopsy, by Hospital Officer, GRATUITOUS ; WHO IS SUCH OFFICER (see Ham., p. 613).—Under the Coroners' Act of 1887 (50 and 51 Vict. Ch., 71), the medical officer of a public hospital is not entitled to remuneration for making a post-mortem upon a patient dying therein whom it was his duty to attend, or for testifying in regard thereto.

Held, that a children's and general hospital, supported by voluntary contributions and founded for free admission of patients within a certain area, and admission for small fees of those within another area, is a public hospital within the meaning of said Act.

Held, also, that a medical man practising in the neighborhood of the public hospital and appointed honorary medical
officer thereof, although receiving no fees or honorarium, is a
medical officer of a public hospital, and as such entitled to no
fees for making an autopsy or testifying in the case of a person dying therein.

Horner *v.* Lewis, 67 L.J.R., Q.B.Div., 524.

Non-Payment of Fees DOES NOT EXCUSE WITHHOLDING
DEATH CERTIFICATE.—A registered medical practitioner refused
a certificate of the cause of child's death because 12*s.*, alleged
to be due him as fees, were unpaid. The child's father called
seven times for the certificate; and eight days after, the coroner, to prevent public scandal, held an inquest. The doctor
was fined 40*s.* and costs, amounting in all to £5 9*s.* 6*d.*

London *Law Times,* April 2, 1898, vol. civ., p. 501.

Arbitration of Fees FOR SERVICES TO WORKINGMEN.—In
England, under Workmen's Compensation Act of 1897, application for arbitration of medical fees in cases of deceased workmen may be made under Workmen's Compensation Rules,
1898.

Weekly *Notes,* June 18, 1898, p. 213.

Held, in Maryland, that a faith-curer could not recover for
his services—per Wright, J.

Doty *v.* Winters, Oct. 27, 1897 (*supra*).

III. Malpractice.

Who are Liable in Action for Malpractice.—If A., holding
himself out as a physician, is employed by B. in the belief that
he is qualified in that capacity, and thereupon undertakes to
treat B. as a physician, he is liable for injuries resulting from
his practice, according to the same standard required by the
law of qualified physicians.

Matthei *v.* Wooley, 69 Ill. App., 654.

Hospitals (Ham., p. 613).—A. went as a pay patient to a
hospital in New York city, maintained as a charitable institution, and was there operated upon by B., her private physician as well as visiting surgeon on the hospital staff. While
still under ether, she was carried to her room and placed in a
bed, from which the nurse in attendance had neglected to
remove an uncovered hot-water bag. Her right leg was burned

so badly as to necessitate an operation. Her sister had made special arrangements for a trained nurse at $3 a day. The nurse whose carelessness led to the injury had entered the institution eight months before, begun a two-years' course of instruction, been instructed in the use of hot-water bags, and given satisfaction in other surgical cases. A. sued the hospital for damages.

Held (at trial term, dismissing the complaint and refusing to plaintiff a new trial), that the case was one of tort, not contract, and that defendant was liable only for negligence in the original selection of its servants, but not for their subsequent acts if they were properly chosen—unless knowledge of the servant's unfitness was brought home to the corporation; the institution being of a charitable nature, notwithstanding it received pay patients, since the money of the latter went to support the hospital and not to make dividends.

As to whether a charitable hospital is liable for negligence in selection of nurses other than the head nurse,—Query?

Ward v. St. Vincent's Hospital, 23 Misc., 91.

Question for Jury—WHAT KNOWLEDGE, SKILL, CARE, AND JUDGMENT ARE REQUIRED?—(Ham., p. 605; vol. ii., pp. 573–583).—The facts of the following case, stated with unusual detail by the court, are substantially as follows: On May 2, 1888, A., forty-four years old, in good health, fractured the right patella. He drove two and one-half miles to the office of B., a physician and surgeon, in whose absence B.'s father, also a physician and surgeon, applied strips of adhesive plaster on each side of the calf, running them over the knee to the thigh, bandaged the leg, applied a splint eighteen inches long, and bandaged again. A. walked to his wagon and drove home over a rough road. On the way, bandage and splint loosening, A. at home, with his wife's aid, tightened them as best he could. On May 8th, nothing having been done meantime, A. sent for B. and told him what his father had done and what happened subsequently. The knee was then swollen to the thigh's size. B. removed bandages and splint, examined the hurt, diagnosed it as rupture of the ligaments, and bade plaintiff lie quietly in bed until they united, which might take eight weeks. Bandages and splint were off for half an hour, while B. measured both legs with tape and rule, finding half an inch difference. B. washed the

parts, and replaced the bandages and splints about as his father
had done—not in the 8-shape nor by attaching the bandages to
the splint's ends.   No means were used to steady the leg below
the splint; but, after placing the foot on some cushions resting
upon a board at the bed's foot, B. departed, promising to return
with a longer, better splint.   He returned three days after,
removed splint and bandages, treated the leg for about half an
hour, bathed it in warm water, restored the bandages, and
applied a splint reaching farther up the leg and down to the
heel, where he wrapped the outer bandage around the foot and
fastened it; the leg being still swollen, nothing was done to
reduce the swelling except as stated.   In all, B. made five
visits—two the first week, and the others on May 26th and 30th
and June 7th.   On the last day he put back the short splint
and told A. that he might go about his business as assessor,
but to be careful not to hurt the leg, as if he, A., were thrown
from his wagon or hurt by his own negligence, he, B., did not
wish to be responsible.   B. also said A. might walk about the
house with the short splint on.   A. did so walk, and went out
two or three days in a buggy on his business; during which
time, he said, his leg was not injured, his heel resting, while
driving, upon boards arranged on the dash-board.   The roads
were rough and likely to cause jolting, and B. knew their condition.   At no time were efforts made to unite the patella's
fracture.   The strips of adhesive plaster first applied remained
until June 15th, when A. calling pursuant to directions at B.'s
office, B. removed them, and, without trying to keep the parts of
the patella together, tried to flex the still swollen leg, washed it,
put it in the short splint again, saying that ligamentous union
had begun, gave a liniment for use, bade A. work and flex the
leg, showed him how to apply the splint and bandages, but
gave no directions as to how to keep the patella's parts together
while working the leg.   Thereafter nothing was put on except
the short splint and bandage.   B. made no objection to A.'s
going about his business, but said the leg was doing well.   On
the following Saturday A. called at B.'s office again, where B.
treated the leg as before: took it across his knee, tried to work
it, said if it didn't loosen up he would give A. ether and
"break the damn thing down," and bade A. use skunk's oil—
which A. did; whereafter the knee "began to loosen up some,"
and the upper part of the patella "began to slip up some."

About July 15th, A. told B. that his leg was not set right, as there was space between the parts of the patella. B. read from a surgical work to prove that it was all right. In August A. asked if he could do haying, and B. said it would hurt him no more, if he was careful, than walking around. A. therefore rode on the mowing machine a few days, being careful not to hurt his leg. From June 15th until the splint's removal in September, A. visited B.'s office, and was told every time that the leg was doing well. About March 1, 1889, A., learning from another surgeon that the patella was fractured, again told B. that the leg was not set right. B., on examination, admitted for the first time that the knee-cap was broken, and later in the spring said to A. that "the leg was not worth a damn, and he would have to go into something else besides farming."

A. brought an action against B. to recover damages for malpractice, testified that the leg still at the time of trial hurt very much in driving; that he could work very little on the farm, and could not walk on rough ground without turning the ankle, or plough, drag, or walk on ploughed ground to any extent; that he could not lift half so much as before the accident, and not lift at all unless he stood straight; that he could not hold his leg up; that he was informed by physicians that there was no ligamentous union; and that, relying upon B.'s statement that the leg was getting on all right, he had not consulted any other physician. Expert testimony went to show that while fracture of the patella is not common, rupture of the ligaments connected with it is very uncommon; that powerful muscles extending from its upper and lower portions hold it in place, which muscles cannot be controlled by strips of adhesive plaster if the leg is flexed; that in treating the injury it is necessary to know what it is, and to reduce the swelling; that a fractured patella might be united if there were some swelling, but with difficulty if a knee was swollen as large as a thigh, when it would be hard to know if the parts had been brought together or not; that in such a fracture, broken parts should be placed and kept in apposition, the patient remaining perfectly quiet for eight or ten weeks until strong ligamentous union takes place, and thereafter the leg should be used very carefully until the ligaments grow strong enough not to rupture; that a splint should be used as soon as possible, and not changed for some time, so as to prevent separation of the bony parts, and not removed during examinations, which should be frequent, to ascertain whether reseparation has occurred; that the leg should not be flexed for eight or ten weeks; that when flexed the patella should be supported in both directions by pressure; that the splints should be kept on for about a year—the long splint for two or three months, and thereafter a short one; that a splint from the centre of the thigh to the middle of the leg would not serve to keep the leg quiet; that the patient should not work or use the leg much for a year, or do active work for a year and a half; that it would be contrary to practice to allow one sustaining such a fracture in May to assist at harvest wearing a short splint or to ride over rough roads in June, as such action would probably break up adhesions; that it was contrary to usual practice after putting on a long splint to remove it, leaving the patella and leg without other support than adhesive plaster; and that there should be pressure when the bandages are removed. It appeared at the time of trial that the fractured parts were 2 ½ inches apart when the leg was flexed, and 1 ½ when extended; that neither bony nor ligamentous union had taken place; and that the result was bad, although in such cases it is usually good.

There was of course conflict in evidence, but the court considered that the jury might have found legitimately the facts as above stated, if taking the view of it most favorable to plaintiff, as the court was obliged to do—the complaint having been dismissed at trial. The Court of Appeals, therefore, upon the ground that the conflict of evidence presented facts for the determination of the jury, reversed the judgment and ordered a new trial, saying that "the law relating to malpractice is simple and well settled, although not always easy of application" ; that a physician is bound to possess "that reasonable degree of learning and skill that is ordinarily possessed by physicians and surgeons in the locality where he practises, and which is ordinarily regarded by those cognizant of the employment as necessary to qualify him to engage in the business of practising medicine and surgery" ; that he is bound to exercise and apply his skill and learning to accomplish the purpose of his employment, and to use his best judgment in so doing, being liable in law for injuries resulting from failure to fulfil any of these obligations; that he need not possess extraordinary learning and skill, but only that degree possessed by the

average member of his profession in good standing—being
bound, however, to keep abreast of the times, and at the same
time liable for injuries resulting from "a departure from approved methods in general use," however good his intentions;
that he need not exercise the highest degree of care ever exercised, either by himself or others, providing that he does exercise ordinary and reasonable care; that while he must exercise
his best judgment after careful examination, he is not liable
for a mere error of judgment; and, finally, that his contract is
not to guarantee good results, but "to use the skill and learning
of the average physician, to exercise reasonable care and to
exert his best judgment in the effort to bring about a good
result."

Pike *v.* Honsinger, 155 N. Y., 201.

(The above case has been stated thus fully as being the latest
utterance of the New York Court of Appeals upon this topic of
vital interest to medical men.   The cases cited by the court
are, with one exception, among those cited in Hamilton (pp.
605, 606), and if any criticism may be ventured, it is that the
use by the learned court of the words "in the locality where he
practises" is misleading—as was pointed out in Gramm *v.*
Boener, 56 Ind., 497 (Ham., p. 606); for it is very possible
that the defendant in a malpractice case might be the only
practitioner in his locality; or, although grossly incompetent,
even by the standard of similar localities, he might be superior
to other practitioners of his neighborhood.   The Court of Appeals, however, seems to have negatived this unfortunate
phrase by its subsequent holding that the standard is the qualification of "the average member of the medical profession in
good standing."

In an Iowa case, Whitesell *v.* Hill, 101 Iowa, 629; 70 N.W.,
750 (April, 1897), it was held that, while the correct rule is
that a physician should possess the skill, etc., of the average
practitioner in *similar localities* to that of his practice, nevertheless to charge that he should have the skill, etc., of the
profession "generally in the vicinity of where the defendant
practised," was not reversible error, in this particular case, because it appeared in evidence that several educated and experi-
enced physicians practised in defendant's neighborhood.)

So as to Dentistry.—In North Carolina, a month later
than Pike's case (April, 1898), it was held that a dentist must

exercise the care and skill of the profession generally, and not of his particular locality only.

McCracken v. Smathers, 29 S.E., 354.

A case somewhat resembling Pike v. Honsinger in its facts, and involving the same legal principles, was decided shortly before (in December, 1897), by the Supreme Court of Nebraska. On July 4, 1890, plaintiff fractured the patella, and immediately called Dr. A., who dressed the wound and applied a temporary splint. Plaintiff was taken home, and at night called Dr. B., who applied adhesive plasters to the knee, put it in roller bandages and a fracture-box, and continued to visit and treat plaintiff. On July 7th Dr. B. requested Drs. C. and D. to examine the wound, and one of them advised making incisions in the skin and flesh of the knee and binding the fractured parts together with silver wire; and on July 10th, in company with B. and a layman, C. and D. performed the operations, in the course of which, owing to a movement of plaintiff's leg, one of them broke a drill, its point being left in the knee-cap. On July 14th, 22d, and 25th, and Aug. 1st, but not after the last date, C. and D. visited plaintiff, who did not get well until the spring of 1891, when other surgeons performed an operation. He brought action against C. and D., and at trial established permanent injury, viz., shrinkage of the muscles of the thigh and leg, and stiffness and enlargement of knee-joint. Upon appeal from a judgment for defendants—

Held, that the evidence being conflicting, it was properly for the jury to decide the following issues: (1) Whether defendants promised (a) to make a perfect cure, (b) to continue in attendance until plaintiff should recover. (2) Whether the wiring method was proper; on which issue, experts, as usual, testified on both sides. (3) Whether it was negligent to leave the piece of drill in the bone; on this issue, also experts testified—some that the practice was improper, and others that, owing to the inflamed condition of the knee, plaintiff's high temperature, and rapid pulse, the fragment could not have been removed without danger of breaking the bone; and therefore, as it was well antisepticized, to leave it was proper. (4) Whether it was negligent not to inform plaintiff that the drill's point was in his knee; on this issue the jury found that defendants in good faith believed that the fragment's presence would not harm the knee, if plaintiff were ignorant of it, whereas if he knew of it his anxiety might work injury; and this being so, the mere fact that they were mistaken in opinion was not ground to hold them negligent as matter of law. And the court laid down the rule of law that surgeons are not held to a standard of infallibility, or required to use the utmost possible skill and care, but that they need exercise only "that degree of knowledge and skill ordinarily possessed by members of their profession." Other issues involved related to legal practice, and are not of medical interest.

Van Skike *v.* Potter, 73 N.W., 295.

Duty to Inform Patient of Misadventures.—A., performing a surgical operation, broke a needle, and failed, after careful search, to find a fragment. Subsequently he had to abandon the case, and did so without informing the patient or her friends that the fragment remained in her body. The patient thereafter suffering much pain, another practitioner, operating to remove cicatricial tissue, found the fragment encysted and harmless. There was testimony that the patient's pain could not have resulted from the presence of the encysted needle. The jury were instructed that a physician is only bound to possess, display, and exercise the knowledge, skill, and care usual among medical men of good standing in his community.

Held, that a verdict for defendant should be sustained.

Eislein *v.* Palmer, 7 Ohio Dec., 365; *cf.* Van Skike *v.* Potter (*supra*).

Whether Liability in Damages Arises from a Mistake, Is a Question for the Jury.—A., after treating B. at intervals from October, 1896, to May, 1897, for malady of his right leg, advised an operation. B. went to hospital on May 11th. On May 12th a nurse shaved and prepared the right leg for an operation at B.'s direction, and a hospital surgeon administered chloroform. Both legs were affected and swollen. In the operating-room, A. said that the wrong leg had been prepared, and directed the preparation of the left leg. He asked B.'s brother which leg was to be operated on. The latter said he did not know, but would telephone to his folks. A. said all right. Meantime B.'s father came to the hospital, and A., pointing to the right leg, said: "Is that the right leg?" The father answered: "No; the other leg." Whereupon A. operated upon the left leg. B., coming out of the anæsthesia, was

asked by A. what leg he wished operated on, and said the
right. A. answered: "I thought it was the left; you told me
downstairs it was the left." B. suffered much pain from the
left leg after the operation. Five weeks later, A. operated
upon the right leg, which gave no pain after the operation.
B. sued A. for negligence, and the court directed a verdict for
defendant.

Held, reversing the judgment, that it was for the jury to say
whether upon the facts A. had exercised due care.

Sullivan *v.* McGraw, 76 N.W., 149 (Mich.).

Abandonment of the Case.— Where plaintiff alleged an
agreement to visit and treat him until recovery.

Held, that under a general denial, defendants might show
that upon their last visit they told plaintiff that they would
not return unless requested to do so, and that they had not been
so requested.

Van Skike *v.* Potter (*supra*).

Proximate Cause—Obstetrics.—A. delivered B. of a five-
months fœtus on Oct. 29, 1891, and attended her until Nov.
20th. On Oct. 30th he removed the placenta, but left, as B.
alleged, a piece 2 inches long and ⅔ of an inch thick, which
putrified and produced blood-poisoning and a septic condition
resulting in gangrene of the left leg, which had to be ampu-
tated. The piece of afterbirth was found at the mouth of the
womb and removed by another physician, three weeks after
delivery. B. sued A., and her action was dismissed on the
ground that there was (*a*) no evidence when blood-poisoning
commenced; (*b*) no proof that she would not have lost her leg
if all the afterbirth had been removed; (*c*) that failure to remove it was not negligence.

Held, reversing judgment for defendant, that upon the evidence the question of negligence was for the jury.

Moratzsky *v.* Wirth, 67 Minn., 46; 69 N.W., 480 (Dec.,
1896).

(Although the above case is reported in December, 1896, it
again recurs in the reports under date of Nov. 3, 1898, upon the
point of expert evidence (see that head *infra*). The new trial
granted as above resulted in a verdict of $1,800 for the plain-
tiff, which was sustained on appeal, although the court admitted
that a verdict for the defendant might have been properly
rendered. 76 N.W., 1,032.)

Proximate Cause — Anæsthetics. — B. and C. undertook to reduce a dislocation of A.'s shoulder, and administered to him chloroform, under the influence of which he died. A.'s administratrix having brought an action to recover damages for alleged malpractice, the court found the main question to be: "Did the deceased die from suffocation produced by the use of an undue quantity or excessive dose of chloroform or from its improper administration?" At the operation only the physicians and decedent's son were present, and their testimony was contradictory to his. The only expert physician called by the plaintiff answered to a hypothetical question, summarizing the son's testimony, that he could not assign the cause of death. A physician attending the autopsy and called by defendant was of opinion that death resulted from calcareous degeneration of the heart, but said it might have been due to the shock and pain, or to an overdose of chloroform. Two other physicians were of opinion from the condition of the lungs that death did not result from suffocation or strangulation, but from calcareous degeneration. Verdict for plaintiff.

Held, on appeal, reversing the judgment, that upon the testimony the most that could be said was that the cause of death was doubtful, and attributable as much to one cause as to another, and, therefore, that plaintiff had failed to sustain the burden upon her of proving that the proximate cause of death was the negligence or malpractice of defendants.

Yaggle *v.* Allen, 24 App. Div., 594; cf. Moratsky *v.* Wirth, *infra*, under head of " Experts."

Contributory Negligence—Dentists. ELEMENTS OF DAMAGE.—In her action for damages A. alleged two acts of dental malpractice: (1) Filling upon a live nerve without proper packing; (2) improperly and unnecessarily boring through the jaw-bone after plaintiff had returned for treatment. Defendant asked the court to charge that if the jury found that defendant had advised plaintiff to return for treatment if the tooth troubled her, and she did not do so, such disregard of instructions was negligent on her part and she could not recover; the court so charged, adding: " Provided the defendant used ordinary skill and his best judgment."

Held, affirming judgment for plaintiff, that plaintiff's negligence could not have caused the injuries, that the question of her contribution to them was fairly put to the jury, and that if a practitioner fail to have and exercise proper knowledge, skill, and care according to his best judgment, the patient's neglect to obey his instructions at most only mitigates damages, but does not afford a full defence to the action for malpractice.

Held, also, that the question whether, if a patient failed to obey instructions to return within a week, it was the dentist's duty to seek him, or at what times the relation of physician and patient ceases, was too general and inadmissible.

Held, also, that in assessing damages the jury might consider the patient's pain, loss of time, permanence of injury, delay in effecting cure, and loss of teeth.

McCracken *v.* Smathers, 29 S.E., 354.

Measure of Damages AS AFFECTED BY PATIENT'S REFUSAL TO SUBMIT TO AN OPERATION. RIGHT OF PATIENT SO TO REFUSE.—A., injured by a fall in the street, sued the city. It appeared that on the morning after his accident the hospital surgeon advised an operation for hernia, and A. admitted that in refusing it he was mistaken. Defendant contended that the refusal was unreasonable, and at its request the court charged the jury that if the plaintiff declined to act upon the advice of the house surgeon and submit to an operation for the radical cure of his hernia, the defendant was not chargeable with the consequence of his refusal.

Held, sustaining judgment for plaintiff, that this statement of the law was more favorable to defendant than needful; that "the plaintiff was not required to submit blindly to professional advice. He was entitled and bound to exercise reasonable judgment; and if his conduct was that of a reasonably prudent man, he was within his rights in refusing to submit to an operation, and cannot be charged with negligence in that respect."

Williams *v.* City of Brooklyn, 33 App. Div., 539.

Evidence in Malpractice and Negligence Cases—A physician who has examined plaintiff may testify (1), as matter of opinion, that the latter could not well have feigned his illness, or, without the use of chloroform, have sustained an operation that was performed; and (2), as matter of fact, that plaintiff was confined to his bed and unable to walk without aid.

M. K. & T. Ry. Co. *v.* Wright, 47 S.W., 56 (Texas).

So in an action charging surgical malpractice in the amputation of plaintiff's leg, non-expert witnesses may testify as to their observations of the leg's condition, so long as they confine themselves to statements of fact and do not express opinions.

Williams *v.* Nally, 45 S.W., 874 (Ky).

(See below under title "Evidence," sub-title "Experts.")

Evidence of Medical Qualifications.—It is not allowable to show a physician's incompetency by proof of improper treatment of particular cases. His reputation for skill or lack of it must be shown by the testimony of persons who know what that reputation is in the community wherein he practises.

Lacy *v.* Kossuth Co., 75 N.W., 689 (Iowa).

PLEADING.—Although plaintiff fail to allege in an action of malpractice his own freedom from negligence, the defect is cured if subsequent pleadings present that issue.

Williams *v.* Nally, 45 S.W., 874 (*supra*).

IV. Evidence.

Privilege of Professional Confidences. (Ham. pp. 616–632).—A., having fallen in a village street, brought an action to recover damages for alleged resulting injuries, viz., umbilical hernia, prolapsus uteri, and divers bruises. Defendant sought to show by B., her physician, that she had umbilical hernia before the action. B. testified that what he knew of her condition he had learned while attending her in his professional capacity, and that such information was necessary to enable him easily and understandingly to treat the case. His attendance had lasted over eight or ten years, including two cases of childbirth. Defendant's counsel contended that if B. discovered the hernia while attending in childbirth, but did not treat the patient for it or need his knowledge of it to enable him to deliver the child, the statutory privilege did not attach to the information, and the doctor might testify. The trial court excluded his testimony, and upon appeal from a judgment of $2,500 in A.'s favor—

Held, that the evidence was properly excluded, B. having acquired his information while acting in a professional capacity, and the discovery of the hernia being a necessary incident of the investigation made to enable him to act in that capacity.

Nelson *v.* Village of Oneida, 156 N. Y., 219.

(*Cf.* to the same purport, Lammiman *v.* Detroit Citizens' Ry. Co., 71 N.W., 153 Mich., May, 1897).

A. sued as administrator to recover damages for his intestate's death from injuries due to a fall on the city's street. Decedent was attended by several physicians, one of whom A. called as plaintiff's witness. Defendant then called the others to testify as to decedent's condition.

Held, that under the Iowa code the testimony of defendant's said witnesses as to what information they obtained in treating decedent was properly excluded; as was also a question addressed to one of them, asking if decedent had not inquired of him whether the injury to her hip might not have been due to another cause.

> Baxter *v.* City of Cedar Rapids, 103 Iowa, 599; 72 N.W., 790 (October, 1897).

All statements made to a physician and necessary to enable him to treat a patient intelligently are privileged communications.

> Kenyon *v.* City of Mondovi, 73 N.W., 314 (Wisc.).

Communications by a Prisoner Not Privileged. — Defendant, charged with murder, was attended medically in prison by A. up to the day before the latter was called as a witness.

Held, that A. might testify as to conversation with defendant, after the termination of his professional relations, upon topics not relating to defendant's health, and as to differences between the appearance of defendant in and out of court.

> People *v.* Koerner, 154 N. Y., 355.

Decedent's Estate. — In an action against a decedent's estate to recover the value of services, the testimony of a physician upon that issue is not competent, if his testimony was acquired in attendance upon deceased in a professional capacity.

> Re Johnson, 32 App. Div., 634.

(The above proposition is stated broadly in the opinion, but the court held that its rulings upon other points obviated the need of passing upon this one. Its expression, therefore, may be regarded as obiter. Under sec. 834 of the code, it is not sufficient to make information privileged that it should have been acquired in professional attendance, unless also *necessary to enable the physician to act in his professional capacity.*)

A. sued B., a trust company, and temporary administrator of a deceased patient, to recover $24,700, less a small credit, which plaintiff alleged was owing to him for medical services rendered to decedent and her husband for a period of sixteen months. A. did not offer to testify himself as to these services, but sought to establish his claim by the testimony of one C., who during the time referred to attended decedent daily as medical adviser. C., although a licensed physician, had never registered pursuant to the public health law of New York, and therefore was not legally qualified to practise medicine. This disqualification, plaintiff claimed, took C. out of the category of physicians, who are forbidden to reveal professional confidences, and rendered him a competent witness for the plaintiff. But the learned trial court excluded his testimony upon these grounds, stated in a written opinion refusing an application for a new trial. The relations of C., the witness, to decedent were professional and confidential. The questions asked of C., under objection, "called for a statement by him of information obtained in his professional capacity, either directly from the patient herself or by observation, and were clearly inadmissible." The fact that C. had not complied with the registration law only affected him personally, rendering him liable to punishment for violation of this statute. The patient had a right to presume that her physician was lawfully practising, and the privilege, being hers, could not be waived or abrogated by the fact that C. was practising contrary to law. To bring a witness within the statute it is sufficient that he has attended as a physician upon the patient, and in that capacity obtained, as necessary to treat the case, the information sought to be elicited. The learned court thus stated the purpose of the law: "The statute was not passed for the pecuniary benefit of the medical fraternity, but to silence its voice, and in this manner protect those seeking medical assistance, by excluding all inquiries which may offend the sensitiveness of the living or reflect in the slightest on the memory of the dead. It was to throw the mantle of charity over the sick and unfortunate, and at the same time elevate the medical practitioner to the high plane with the clergy and Good Samaritan, leaving him to protect his fees according to professional ethics, so long as he does not infringe the humanitarian sentiment embraced in the statutory prohibition."

McGillicuddy *v.* Farmers' Loan & Trust Co., *N. Y. Law Journal*, Jan. 11, 1899.

4

(Although the above decision was rendered at trial term by a single judge, McAdam, J., the reputation of its author for precision, his long experience, and careful review of cases, entitle it to more weight than is sometimes given to *nisi prius* opinions. The leading cases relied upon will be found cited in Hamilton. It would appear from the opinion that the witness C. was allowed to testify that he saw plaintiff in decedent's house, and to state the number of times he saw him there. What he was not permitted to recite was what occurred in the privacy of the sick chamber; and the rule as laid down in this opinion seems to be that in such a case a physician may testify for another to the latter's employment by the patient, the number of his visits, examinations, prescriptions, and operations; and, if objection be made to describing the operations, then to their value. But he may not testify as to the nature of the sickness, or to anything learned by him in his confidential relations and necessary to proper treatment of the case.)

Effect of Refusal TO REVEAL PLAINTIFF'S CONFIDENCE IN AN ACTION BY THE PHYSICIAN.—In a Scotch case, where a physician insured against blood-poisoning under an accident policy claimed damages on the ground that he had been poisoned by the virus of a syphilitic female patient whose name he refused to disclose, it was held that this refusal justified a non-suit. This case is noted editorially in the *Albany Law Journal*, June 9, 1897, and is not cited from the reports.

Waiver of Privilege (Ham., p. 626).—A. fell on the broken stairway of a club-house and brought an action to recover damages for resulting injuries. She testified to the hospital treatment by physicians, and on cross-examination to the physician's name. The defence then called the physician and asked his diagnosis; plaintiff's counsel objected, and the court ruled "that her conversation with the doctor being brought out on cross-examination of the defendant's counsel, and being questioned she was obliged to answer, she herself had no privilege, does not open the door to waive the privilege of her physician to refrain from disclosing what he had learned by private examination of his patient." [Here the learned court apparently fell into error, for the privilege is not the physician's, but the patient's. Were it the former's, he might waive it against the patient's wish.] Subsequently the court said: "My ruling is that you are not entitled to obtain from this witness a disclosure of what he ascertained by an examination of this woman while she was his patient." On appeal from a judgment of $3,200—

Held, that as A. in her testimony in chief went very fully into her treatment at the hospital and the various operations performed upon her, she thereby waived her privilege; that such waiver must be determined, as a question of fact, from the acts of the plaintiff during the trial; that one of two principles must be adopted in this class of cases—either plaintiffs shall be allowed to testify to what happened while under treatment and no testimony allowed to contradict them, or else their testimony must be considered to be a waiver of privilege. In the former event a plaintiff would be entirely safe in testifying to anything, the mouths of the only persons able to contradict the testimony being closed.

Rauh *v.* Deutsche Verein, 29 App. Div., 483; N. Y. S., 985.

(The above important case was decided in the Appellate Division, First Department, by a divided court of three to two—two of the majority and one dissenting judge writing opinions. The result arrived at does not seem fairly reconcilable with Nelson *v.* Oneida Village (*supra*), which was not cited, or in accord with Western decisions. In the dissenting opinion the learned judge said: "Can it be said, while the statute above referred to" (Code, sec. 834) "remains in force, that if a person sustains an injury and thereafter brings an action to recover damages therefor, because he testifies in his own behalf to the injury sustained, and that he was treated by a physician who gave him medicine and who performed an operation, he thereby waives the privilege accorded by the statute? I think not. Such a conclusion seems to me absurd. It is true a waiver may be inferred from circumstances, but there must be something present from which it can be at least inferred that the party waiving does so willingly, voluntarily, purposely, and intentionally." The learned dissenting judges considered that if the rule worked hardship, the remedy was with the legislature, and not with the courts.)

Later the Second Division held without dissent, in an action by A. to recover damages for a libelous publication imputing to her insanity, that by calling a physician to prove that, at the time when the libel alleged her to be in Bellevue

Hospital, she was, in fact, in St. John's Hospital, suffering
from an illness the nature of which would have prevented her
from leaving the latter place, the plaintiff waived her privilege,
and upon cross-examination defendant was entitled to ask the
physician the nature of her malady.

Lawson *v.* Morning Journal Ass'n., 32 App. Div., 71 ;
52 N.Y.S., 484.

But in Iowa it was held that the plaintiff in a negligence
case did not, by calling her physician as a witness, waive her
privilege so as to permit other physicians, in attendance on her
and called by defendant, to testify as to her condition.

Baxter *v.* City of Cedar Rapids (*supra*).

Under the California code, a physician cannot be examined
in a civil action as to the necessary information acquired in
treating a patient; but if he give such testimony without objection by the patient, it cannot be stricken out, and the latter will
be held to have waived his objection; but *semble* that, although
the patient has testified to what took place by way of medical
treatment, he can still by timely objection close the physician's
mouth.

Lissak *v.* Crocker Estate Co., 119 Cal., 442 ; 51 P., 688.

Privilege of Patients IS NOT THAT OF A HORSE OR HIS
OWNER.—A., an attorney, telegraphed for a veterinary to come
immediately to attend his sick horse, Bravo. The telegram
was delayed five hours, and Bravo died in consequence, as was
alleged, of this delay. A. sued the telegraph company, which
on cross-examination asked the veterinary what plaintiff had
said as to the reports on the horse's condition. This was
objected to, amusingly enough, and, amazing to say, the trial
court sustained the objection, on the ground that the matter
was privileged.

Held, on appeal, that the provisions of the Iowa code as to
privileged communication to physicians do not apply to veterinary surgeons.

Hendershott *v.* West. Union Tel. Co., 76 N.W., 828.

(When it is considered that the purpose of "privilege" is to
permit a patient to reveal to the medical man physical conditions that, except for this privilege, might be concealed even
at the risk of death or injury, the humor of extending it to a
horse or his owner is obvious and delightful.)

Dying Declarations.—Dying declarations are still competent in evidence under the New York Criminal Code. But it is erroneous to charge a jury that " it is the experience of mankind that the premonition of immediate death, from which there is no hope of recovery, is always sufficient to influence persons so situated to tell the truth "; for this substantially instructs jurors that if the statement were untrue it would be the first instance on record where a dying declaration had been false.

People *v.* Corey, 157 N. Y., 332; 51 N.E., 1,024.

Under the Georgia Penal Code a writing signed by deceased *in articulo*, with knowledge of his condition, is admissible as a dying declaration, if there be evidence that it was read to him, that he understood its contents, and intended it to be such declaration. It is for the jury to say what weight will attach to it under the circumstances.

Perry *v.* State, 30 S.E., 903.

Decedent, having said she was going to die, made a certain statement, and, a few minutes after it was made, again said that she was going to die.

Held, that this statement was admissible in evidence as a dying declaration.

State *v.* Trusty, 40 Atl., 766.

Under the Pennsylvania statute, dying declarations of a woman on whom defendant is alleged to have committed abortion are inadmissible in evidence, unless the prosecution has by satisfactory and competent evidence proved her soundness of mind when they were made.

Held, that such declarations might be received upon the testimony of the physician in charge that deceased, when roused from a state of coma shortly subsequent to such declarations and a few hours before death, replied to questions intelligently.

Commonwealth *v.* Keene, Weekly Notes of Cases (Pa.), vol. xlii, p. 567.

To render dying declarations admissible, decedent must have known that he was *in extremis* and have given up all hope of life; but this mental attitude may be shown not only by what he said, but by his danger and the surrounding circumstances.

Jones *v.* Commonwealth, 46 S.W., 217; 20 Ky. L.R., 355. (*Cf.* In re Orpen, 86 Fed. R., 760.)

Mental Weakness—INCOMPETENCY.—Upon a petition to have a person declared incompetent, a physician testified thus: " From his appearance, and questions asked and answered by

Mr. ——, and his actions, I should judge he would be a man
of feeble mind. I would not like to use the word ' unsound.' "
Another physician testified that in his "judgment," —— was
very much "demented." Upon cross-examination he explained
that by this he meant to say, "his mind is weakened"; and
being further asked, "Is that all you will say—that his mind
is weakened?" answered "Yes." The court held that proof
of mere weakness of mind not amounting to imbecility is insufficient, and that it was erroneous to allow the question to
be put to the two physicians, whether in their opinion the
alleged incompetent is a man unable to take care of himself
and his affairs.

    In re Rush, 53 N. Y., 581.

Extent to which Non-Expert Witness may Testify TO
MENTAL AND BODILY CONDITIONS OF OTHERS.—Lay witnesses
cannot properly give an opinion as to the mental capacity of
A., if that be an issue; but they may state the impressions
produced upon their minds by acts or declarations to which
they have testified, and say whether they regarded those acts as
rational or not.

    Wyse v. Wyse, 155 N. Y., 367; 49 N.E., 942.

Where previous habit of study is essential to the formation
of an opinion, only persons so qualified may testify to such
opinion. But when the subject-matter to which testimony re-
lates cannot be reproduced or described precisely as it was,
non-experts may give opinion-evidence, e.g., to A.'s state of
health; hearing; eyesight; ability to walk, work, or use limbs
naturally; suffering; consciousness; intoxication; excitement;
possession of faculties.

    West Chicago St. Ry. Co. v. Fishman, 169 Ill., 196; 48
    N.E., 447. [Cf. Re McCabe, 40 A., 52 (Vermont).
    Lamb v. Lippincott, 73 N.W., 887 (Mich.). Re
    Christiansen's Estate, 53 Pac., 1,003 (Utah). State
    v. Beuerman, 53 Pac., 874 (Kansas).]

Basis of Expert Testimony.—A plaintiff was seized apparently with an hysterical attack in court. B., a physician present, testified that the seizure was "a form of what is known as
hysteroepileptic or hysteromajor." He was asked: "Now,
doctor, from your experience of Mrs. McGuire, and the facts
stated and testified to here, what do you say was the cause of
that?"

Held, error to have allowed witness to answer this question, as being too vague. Experts must be examined upon hypothetical questions containing the facts assumed to have been proven, so that they may have in mind a definite state of facts. It will not do to refer generally to testimony that has been given.

> McGuire *v.* Brooklyn Heights R.R. Co., 30 App. Div., 227.

Hypothetical questions must contain only facts admitted, established by evidence, or legitimately inferrible by the jury from the evidence.

> Preston *v.* Ocean S.S. Co., 33 App. Div., 193; 53 N.Y.S., 444.

Speculative Testimony.—In an action to recover damages a physician was asked: "Can you tell us with reasonable certainty how long he is apt to have those pains?" And under objection answered: "He may have them during his lifetime."

Held, to be reversible error; that if the question had been, How long will he have those pains?—and the answer had been the same as given, it would still have been too speculative; and, as it was, the form of the question made it even more so.

> Savage *v.* 3d Ave. R.R., 25 Misc., 426 (New York City Court, Gen. Term).

A physician may *not* testify whether decedent was struck from behind or before, unless he describe the wound so minutely that the jury may judge for themselves of the accuracy of his conclusion.

> Parrott *v.* Commonwealth, 47 S.W., 452 (Ky.).

Nor may he testify whether the range of a bullet-wound indicates whether the person firing the shot stood above or below decedent; that not being a matter for expert testimony.

> People *v.* Milner, 54 Pac., 833 (Cal.).

The opinions of experts are to be regarded as conclusive by the jury only when the evidence and facts deducible therefrom are undisputed, and the case concerns a matter of science or specialized art or other matter of which a layman can have no knowledge.

> Moratsky *v.* Wirth, 76 N.W., 1,032.

This is the stoutly litigated obstetrical case above cited, and is interesting to accoucheurs.

Expert Fees. COMPULSORY TESTIMONY (Ham., p. 614).—In a suit for damages against the city of Springfield, A., a physician, subpœnaed as a witness by the city, defendant, was asked a hypothetical question which he refused to answer, thus stating his reason: "On the ground that an expert witness is entitled to a different and greater compensation than an ordinary witness is allowed, and that an expert is not required to give expert testimony without compensation as an expert unless a reasonable compensation shall have been paid or provided for. My reasonable fee for an expert or professional opinion in this case is $10. I have not been paid nor offered anything for compensation for my expert or professional opinion in the case, nor has said compensation been in any way promised to me or provided for. On the contrary, it has been expressly refused. Therefore I decline to testify until such fee is provided for."

Held, that A. was in contempt by his refusal, and properly punishable therefor.

Dixon *v.* The People, 168 Ill., 179; 48 N.E., 108.

(The above case discusses the rule very fully, and is of importance to expert witnesses. For the contrary view, see cases cited in Hamilton; and for other discussion, see editorial of *New York Law Journal*, Dec. 3, 1897.)

X Rays.—In People *v.* Haynes, a case of murder tried Oct. 21, 1897, an *x*-ray photograph was admitted in evidence for the first time in New York, as was said (see *Albany Law Journal*, Oct. 30, 1897). But the *present* editor is of opinion that the *x*-ray process was allowed to be shown in court previously in a negligence case tried in Kings County.

In an action by A. to recover damages for personal injury, where a surgeon testified that he was familiar with the *x*-ray process as well as with fractures, that by aid of those rays he was able to see the fracture and overlapping bones of plaintiff's leg as plainly as if they were uncovered, and that he had taken a photograph offered in evidence, and that it was a fair representation of their condition—

Held, proper to submit the photograph to the jury.

Bruce *v.* Beall, 41 S.W., 445 (Tenn., 1897).

V. Excise Laws and Sales of Intoxicating Liquors (Ham., p. 638).

Liability of Physician for Dispensing.—Under the Missouri statute a practising physician, being a registered pharmacist and owner of a drug-store, cannot sell intoxicating liquor without first writing a prescription therefor.

State *v.* Bailey, 73 Mo. App., 576.

But where a physician, also a registered pharmacist, was indicted for unlawfully selling liquor—

Held, that his own prescription, preserved according to law, although improperly given in that it was for an unnecessary remedy and was a false pretence, constituted a defence.

State *v.* Pollard, 72 Mo. App., 230.

Sales by Pharmacists (Ham., p. 647).—Under the Colorado law it is no defence in an action for selling liquor without a license that the liquor was sold for medicinal purposes.

Chipman *v.* People, 52 Pac., 677.

Under a Colorado ordinance forbidding unlicensed liquor-selling, but in terms not applicable to sales by a druggist upon prescriptions of reputable physicians and for medical purposes—

Held, that a druggist might sell liquor for medical purposes without a prescription.

Prowitt *v.* City of Denver, 52 Pac., 286.

In Georgia, if a medical preparation contains sufficient alcohol to render its sale without license unlawful, the fact that it is sold as medicine is no defence.

Chapman *v.* State, 100 Ga., 311.

A physician accompanied a friend into a drug-shop, and, the two going behind the counter, the physician, in the druggist's presence, poured out two glasses of whiskey, giving one to his friend and drinking the other. After they left the shop the druggist, finding on his counter a prescription by the physician for whiskey, filed it and charged the writer. It was addressed to no one, and in quantity called for " Q. S."

Held, under the Indiana statute, forbidding the sale or gift in drug-shops of whiskey in less quantities than a quart, that the evidence warranted a finding that a gift had been made with the druggist's consent in the intent to evade the statute.

Kyle *v.* State, 18 Ind. App., 136; 47 N.E., 647.

A druggist, licensed to sell liquor without paying the tax of
$50 required by the Kentucky statute, cannot sell liquor un-
mixed with other ingredients, even upon a physician's prescription.

Stormes *v.* Commonwealth, 47 S.W., 262.

In Missouri, pharmacists are not amenable to the dramshop
law. Their sales of intoxicants are governed by the law regulating sales of intoxicating liquors by druggists.

State *v.* Geff, 70 Mo. App., 295.

(*Cf.* State *v.* Coday, 69 Mo. App., 70. State *v.* Williams,
69 Mo. App., 284.)

A physician's prescription cannot render legal a sale made
by him as a pharmacist before it was written.

State *v.* Hale, 72 Mo. App., 78.

Dentists.—Under the North Carolina statute a dentist is
not authorized as a doctor to prescribe whiskey.

State *v.* McMinn, 24 S.E., 523 (1896).

VI. Public Health.

Food : POWER OF AUTHORITIES TO RESTRAIN ITS ADULTERA-
TION AND SALE.

Meat.—The Arkansas statute authorizing cities to prohibit
business dangerous to health does not contemplate as a valid
exercise of such authority the prohibition of the sale of fresh
pork between June and October.

City of Helena *v.* Dwyer, 64 Ark., 424; 42 S.W., 1,071.

The Texas statute prohibiting the sale of food known to be
adulterated in any way, excepting mixtures of ordinary food
which are not injurious to health labelled as mixtures, is invalid because of its vagueness. The particular articles prohibited or required to be labelled should have been enumerated.

Dorsey *v.* State, 44 S.W., 514.

Vinegar.—At common law a person has the right to sell vinegar of any standard not detrimental to health; the New York
Agricultural Law, being in derogation of this right, is to be
strictly construed.

Held, also, that merely to show the existence of less than two
per cent. of cider vinegar solids in a sample of cider vinegar,

without evidence of full evaporation over boiling water in making the test, does not comply with the statutory requirements.
People *v.* Braested, 30 App. Div., 401 ; 51 N.Y.S., 824.

Milk.—The Rhode Island law, forbidding the sale of adulterated or unwholesome provisions for meat or drink, does not apply to the sale of adulterated milk.
State *v.* Luther, 40 A., 9.

A.'s driver carried, from Jersey City to his employer, adulterated milk received in that place from the shipper, which was subsequently returned to the latter.

Held, in the absence of any proof of sale, that the evidence would not sustain an action for the recovery of a penalty under the Agricultural Law of New York, it being improper to presume that the defendant was engaged in an unlawful act.
People *v.* Kellina, 50 N.Y.S., 653.

The Pennsylvania statute, providing that any food shall be deemed adulterated from which any valuable or necessary constituent or ingredient has been wholly or in part extracted—

Held, not to apply to one who sells, as skimmed milk, milk from which cream has been taken by the "centrifugal method," which extracts more cream than ordinary skimming.
Commonwealth *v.* Hufna, 39 Atl., 1,052.

Sale of Milk from Infected Tenements.—A. had a milkshop on the ground floor of a three-story building block of tenements or flats, adapted for separate occupancy and connected by a central stair. He resided on the second floor. The first floor intervening was let separately.

Held, that the place was a building within the Dairies', Cowsheds', and Milkshops' Order of 1885, and that upon the outbreak of an infectious or contagious disease in a family on the second floor, A. should have ceased to sell milk from his shop.
London Co. Council *v.* Edwards (1898), L.R. two Q.B., 75.

Food Adulteration — CASES RELATING TO PLEADING AND PROCEDURE.

State *v.* Luther, 40 Atl., 9 (R. I.). Dorsey *v.* State, 44 S.W., 514 (Texas).

Powers of Municipalities, HEALTH BOARDS, ETC. CONTRACTS.—Under the Indiana statute it is the duty of the county commissioner, acting as a board of health, promptly to act in arresting the spread of contagious diseases. During a small-pox quarantine a township trustee employed A., a watchman, and certified that the amount of his claim for services in that capacity was due.

Held, in a suit by an assignee of said claim, that the county was not liable.

Comm'rs. of Perry Co. *v.* Bader, 50 N.E., 776.

A city's health board may bind the city by its contract to hire premises for hospital uses and for the nursing of the sick.

Turner *v.* City of Toledo, 15 Ohio Cir. Ct. R., 627.

Right of Owners TO NOTICE WHERE TENEMENTS ARE CONDEMNED OR NUISANCES ABATED. DECISIONS OF BOARD NOT JUDICIAL. OWNERS' REMEDIES.—The health board of New York city declared a certain tenement to be unfit for habita-tion and a nuisance, and required the owner to destroy it. The owners sued in equity for the vacation and cancellation of the board's orders and resolution, and that it be enjoined from destroying the premises, alleging that the tenement was not a nuisance or unfit for habitation. Defendants answered that plaintiff had a remedy in the law, that there was no jurisdic-tion in equity, and that the action of said board was taken *bonâ fide* in discharging its duty to preserve the public health. Upon plaintiff's demurrer to the answer—

Held, that there was equitable jurisdiction; that the orders of the board in such cases are not conclusive; that the statutory provision that the action, proceedings, and orders of said board shall be regarded as judicial in nature, does not make the board a court whose orders are final; that the exemption of members of the board from suit or liability for acts done by them in good faith and with ordinary discretion pursuant to its regulations, does not afford a complete defence in such an action, and is demurrable if so pleaded.

Golden *v.* Health Dept., 21 App. Div., 420; 47 N.Y.S., 623.

As the New York statute makes no provision for notice or hearing by the board of health before condemning a tenement as a nuisance, an owner may come into a court of equity to prevent enforcement of the order.

Golden *v.* Health Dept. (*supra*).

A municipal health board need not notify an interested

party of its proceedings to determine a nuisance and order its abatement, since he has a remedy by injunction or against the members of the board personally.

> Hartman *v.* City of Wilmington, 41 Atl., 74.

Under the Arkansas statute, empowering city councils to establish health boards with the duty to secure cities from contagious, malignant, or infectious diseases, such councils have power to authorize such boards to abate nuisances dangerous to health. The statute is valid, and under it the resolution of a health board is not a judicial determination that the property covered by it is a nuisance, nor can such resolution make the property a nuisance.

> Gaines *v.* Waters, 64 Ark., 609; 44 S.W., 353.

Under the Rhode Island law a nuisance caused by a privy vault may be summarily abated; and, therefore, the owner does not have a constitutional right to notice prior to the passage of an order by the aldermen directing him to destroy it.

A statute providing for the destruction of such a vault, pending its owner's appeal from such an order, is constitutional.

So is the provision that failure to comply with such an order within ten days shall subject the owner to a fine of from $5 to $20 a day, and empower the aldermen after sixty days to destroy the vaults.

> Harrington *v.* Board of Aldermen of Providence, 38 Atl., 1.

Unsanitary Tenements. — In New York city a five-story tenement, being 91 feet long and 20 feet wide, with a court from five to seven feet wide, having rear walls eight inches from a dead wall, apartments of three rooms with a single window opening upon an eight-inch court, cellars occupied by sinks, a death-rate abnormally high from unsanitary conditions, and a court entirely surrounded by buildings not less than three stories high—

Held, to be unfit for human habitation.

Held, also, that because such tenement was unfit for habitation, it did not follow necessarily that it should be destroyed, in the absence of proof that it could not be made fit.

Held, also, that the mere fact that the existence of such a tenement, even though uninhabited, renders adjacent buildings unfit for habitation, is not ground for its destruction under the statute.

Held, also, that the fact that such tenement was a nuisance as a habitation was not sufficient ground for its destruction, in the absence of proof that a change of its use would abate the nuisance.

Health Dept. *v.* Dassori, 21 App. Div., 348.

As to procedure under the New York statute for the destruction of tenements—

Health Dept. *v.* Henry De Forest Weeks, N.Y.L.J., Nov. 26, 1897.

Nuisance of Drains. — Under the Public Health Act, Amendments Act, 1890, a drain on private grounds, inaccessible to the public, is a private drain; and if it become a nuisance, local authorities may for its abatement proceed against any owner or premises connected with it by a branch.

Seal *v.* Methyr Tydfil Urban Council, 67 L.J.R., Q.B. Div., 37.

Where a private drain tapping several houses becomes a nuisance, the authorities may serve each owner with a notice addressed to all jointly; and if it is not obeyed, may enter and abate the nuisance at their cost.

Lancaster *v.* Barnes Urban Council, 67 L.J.R., Q.B., 744.

For the rule in the metropolis, see:

Green *v.* Newington vestry (1898), L.R. two Q.B., 1.

The sanitary authorities directed A. and B. to remedy defects of drainage, which it was the duty of said authorities to remedy. A. and B. obeyed. The authorities opposed the recovery of the cost of this work, upon the ground that the notice not being in statutory form, A. and B. were not under legal compulsion to obey it, *i.e.*, were volunteers.

Held, that prompt action being necessary in such cases, and there being little time to consider one's rights, persons doing work under what amounts to compulsion by authorities may recover its cost.

North et al. *v.* Walthamstow Urban Council, 67 L.J., Q.B. Div., 972.

Owners Entitled to Choice of Sanitary Appliances.—A board of health cannot restrict the method of laying a stable floor according to a special plan. Owners have the right to adopt any method that will secure requisite sanitary conditions.

Moreford *v.* Board of Health of Asbury Park, 39 Atl., 706 (N. J.).

A notice by the authorities that a specified kind of water-closet must be substituted for a privy was held invalid, as leaving the owner no choice of equally good closets.

Wood *v.* Widness Corporation, *Law Times*, Feb. 5, 1898, vol. civ., p. 315.

Nuisance of Pest-House—ABANDONMENT OF QUARANTINE SITE (Ham., p. 633).—The city of Baltimore in 1883 destroyed pest-houses theretofore maintained by it outside the city limits, and directed a sale of the land, which remained unused until 1897, when the city put a leper upon the premises.

Held, that the land had been abandoned for quarantine purposes, and could not be used for the detention of the leper to the injury of the adjoining owners, who had improved their land in the belief that the city had abandoned the site for said purposes.

Held, also, that the fact that the pest-house was not originally a nuisance, owing to its remoteness from the city, did not, in the absence of prescriptive right to maintain the establishment, deprive adjacent owners of redress upon the theory that they have come to the nuisance.

Held, also, under the Maryland statute, permitting the establishment of hospitals for the isolation and treatment of contagious diseases, that placing a leper in the home of a private person not a municipal officer is not the establishment of a hospital within the act, and is not justifiable if the caretaker dwells in a settled district; such action on the part of the municipality tending to spread the disease.

City of Baltimore *v.* Fairfield Imp. Co., 39 Atl., 1,081; 40 L.R.A., 494.

Liability of Authorities FOR DAMAGES DUE TO ESTABLISHMENT OF PEST-HOUSE.—The Kentucky statute, which forbids that a pest-house be located near a city or town, and imposes liabilities therefor upon any officer of such city or town, only applies to the executive or ministerial officers who establish the pest-house, but not to legislative officers.

Such an establishment is within the powers of the municipality, which becomes liable in compensatory damages therefor to one injured thereby.

Where the facts stated in a pleading show the existence of a nuisance and damage resulting therefrom to a private person, there is a common-law liability of the municipality to the individual, although there may be no liability under the statute, and the use of the word nuisance is not necessary if the facts alleged show its existence.

Clayton v. City of Henderson, 44 S.W., 667.

A. brought an action against the city of Detroit, to recover damages growing out of the negligence of the city board of health, in permitting to be at large one who had been exposed to small-pox and who came as a guest to A.'s boarding-house.

Held, that the board represented the State, and that the city was not liable.

Gilboy v. City of Detroit, 73 N.W., 128.

Where small-pox broke out upon the premises in the city of Detroit without fault on the part of the board of health, which disinfected and quarantined the house—

Held, that the city was not liable in damages for loss resulting from the infection, and if through negligence of the health officers in performing their work unnecessary damage resulted, any liability therefor devolved upon such officers alone and not upon the city.

Webb v. Board of Health of Detroit, 74 N.W., 734.

Vaccination.—New Vaccination Act of 1898 takes effect Jan. 1, 1899.

Law Times, Aug. 27, 1898, p. 381.   Law Times, Oct.
8, 1898, p. 484.

Compensation of Health Officers (Ham., p. 613).—Under the Kentucky statute, local health boards are entitled to so much compensation for services as the county courts shall in their discretion determine.

Held, that such discretion was judicial, and could not be controlled.

Stephens v. Allard, 44 S.W , 386.

Under the New York statute, authorizing village trustees to make annual appropriations for paying members of health boards fair and just compensation for services—

Held, that in fixing salaries of such members the trustees acted in an administrative or legislative capacity, not judicially, and that their action could not be reviewed by <i>certiorari.</i>

People v. Trustees of Haverstraw, 23 App. Div., 231;
48 N.Y.S., 740.

A local health board contracted with A. during an epidemic for medical services, and audited his bill.

Held, that the board of supervisors could not refuse payment because some of the persons treated by A. were able to pay.

McKillop *v.* Supervisors of Cheboygan, 74 N.W., 1,050 (Mich.).

A., municipal health officer at a monthly salary, claimed to recover as well the value of visits made by him to a small-pox patient. His evidence showed that in one instance he had been authorized by the board of health to employ a physician to make such a visit, but had made it himself. In the other instance the board had directed him to make the visit personally, upon his statement that he would like to make what money there was in it.

Held, that he could not claim extra compensation for these services, since they were embraced within the duties of his office.

Reynolds *v.* City of Mt. Vernon, 26 App. Div., 581; 50 N.Y.S., 473.

Under the Iowa statute a health officer assists in administering the law, but is not required to treat the sick; where, therefore, a health board employed another physician, A., to treat B., affected with a contagious disease, A. is entitled to compensation, even though B. is a pauper and the county has a contract with still another physician to treat its poor.

Lacy *v.* Kossuth County, 75 N.W., 689.

VII. Miscellaneous.

College—Hospitals. Professor's Tenure of Office.—A professor can be removed from the N. Y. P. G. School and Hospital at pleasure by a majority of directors, but upon charges only by a two-thirds vote.

Mandamus is not the remedy for one so removed from the employ of a private corporation.

People ex rel. Kelsey *v.* N.Y.P.G. Med. School and Hospital, 29 App. Div., 244; 51 N.Y.S., 420.

Libel. Right of Privacy—Unauthorized Use of Physician's Name in Advertising Proprietary Articles (Ham., p. 640).—A., manufacturer of a nostrum, "Sallyco," in an advertisement, said: " Dr. B., physician to —— Hospital,

London, and many of the leading physicians, are prescribing
Sallyco as an habitual drink. Dr. B. says: ' Nothing has done
his gout so much good.'"   B. sued A., on the grounds that the
words libelled him in his profession; that they were untrue,
published without his authority or consent, and by their puffing
nature tended to bring him into contempt among medical men
and the laity as guilty of advertising himself, contrary to the
ethical rules of his profession, and thereby to cause him loss
of income. A. admitted the publication was unauthorized, but
denied that its statements were malicious, untrue, or libelous.
On trial it appeared that B. had, in fact, prescribed Sallyco
for patients, to be taken twice daily for a fortnight, and that he
had told A. that he had himself taken it for gout and been
benefited by it. There was no proof of pecuniary damage.
Two questions were left to the jury: (1) Was the matter complained of libelous? (2) If libelous, was it true? The jury,
having found that the matter was not libelous, did not answer
the second question; and the court having reserved the question whether plaintiff upon their finding was entitled to relief,
judgment was given for defendant, the court saying: "The
whole question turns on the meaning of the word ' habitual ' ;
and, I think, when a physician prescribes the daily use of anything for a fortnight at a time, it can hardly be incorrect to say
that he prescribes its habitual use. Assuming that the published matter is true, in fact, the plaintiff is driven to rely on
the admitted fact that the use of his name by the defendant
was unauthorized. He says that he is entitled to an injunction upon it to restrain the defendant from using the plaintiff's
name in the advertisements, on the ground that an injunction
should be granted in every such case where it can be shown
that the use of the plaintiff's name is unauthorized by the
plaintiff, and is calculated to injure him in his profession. I
do not think this is right. It seems to me to be a broader rule
than any which can be extracted from the authorities. I have
been seeking for one more precise and accurate, and I have
come to the conclusion that the proper rule is that stated by
Mr. Witt. In order that an injunction may issue to restrain a
defendant from using a plaintiff's name, the use of it must be
such as to injure the plaintiff's reputation or property. The
jury have found here that its use constitutes no injury to the
plaintiff's reputation. Does it inflict any injury to his prop-

erty? It does not. If the plaintiff was himself the vendor of a rival medicine, it might be different."

Dockrell *v.* Dougall (lxxviii., Law Times, Rep., 840, Q.B.D.; Albany L.J., Sept. 24, 1898; N.Y.L.J., Sept. 29, 1898).

(In New York, Drs. Lewis A. Sayre, J. D. Bryant, Alfred L. Loomis, and F. R. S. Drake, all successfully instituted legal proceedings to stop the unauthorized use of their names by vendors of proprietary remedies in recent times. In each instance, however, the offending parties discontinued the objectionable advertising and settled the cases before trial; none of them are therefore reported. But in the case of the late Sir Morell McKenzie, the Supreme Court of New York did enjoin the unauthorized use of his name to advertise Carlsbad salts (see Ham., p. 643). In view of the fact that members of some medical societies do indorse such remedies without incurring discipline, the weight that a jury would give to the rules of such a society, or their estimate of the damage resulting to one of its members, *qua* member, from such misuse of his name, is at least questionable.)

A. charged that his daughter's sight had been destroyed by B., a physician, through the use of belladonna. B. brought an action to recover for his medical services. A. defended on the ground that B.'s malpractice had caused his daughter's blindness. The jury disagreed. Subsequently A. settled the case, but later published in the newspapers a signed statement, to the effect that the settlement was not a retraction of the charge, which he reiterated, but was made because his pocketbook would not allow him to fight the combination that the doctor had back of him.

B. brought an action in slander and libel, and A. justified, *i.e.*, alleged the truth of his statement. The testimony of all the expert physicians was to the effect that belladonna could not cause blindness; although it appeared that when the loss of vision was first discovered, another physician who was called in expressed an opinion that it was due to the use of that drug, in which opinion B. himself concurred at the time, the loss of vision being then supposed to be temporary. It further appeared that defendant A. had been assured by oculists before suit that it was not possible that his daughter's blindness was due to belladonna.

Held, reversing judgment for defendant, that the justification had failed.

Clemons *v.* Mellon, 27 App. Div., 349.

Literary Property—REPORTS TO PROFESSIONAL BODIES.— A committee of the New Jersey Dental Society, a corporation, made a report on the care and treatment of the teeth, which was read at an annual meeting, accepted, and filed for future discussion; a copy of it was also given to a professional journal, but was not in fact published. A representative of a manufacturing company procured a copy from some one connected with the journal, but without said society's authority, and used excerpts for advertising purposes.

Held, that the mere fact of its reading did not amount to such dedication to the public as would permit an exhibitor to publish it, there being no proof of a general invitation to the public to attend the meeting, or that the auditors did not pay admission.

Dental Society *v.* Denticura Co., 41 Atl., 672 (see N.Y.L.J., Editorial, Dec. 19, 1898).

Manslaughter RESULTING FROM NEGLECT TO AFFORD MEDICAL AID. CHRISTIAN SCIENCE—PECULIAR PEOPLE.—One of the "Peculiar People" was indicted for manslaughter, in that he caused his child's death by withholding medical aid when the infant was ill of bronchitis and pneumonia. The case was tried before Darling, J., and a jury at London Sessions, Sept. 16, 1898. In summing up to the jury, Mr. Justice Darling said: "Not only would he (the prisoner) not call in a doctor, but he left his case to-day absolutely in the hands of the Lord. He did not want any counsel, but said the Lord Jehovah would give a proper verdict; at least, so I understood it. Although the conclave of the Peculiar People has decided that a physician was not to be called in in case of sickness, it had not yet considered the case of a surgeon. The evidence was that none of the Peculiar People had yet had broken bones; but when a case of that kind happened they would have a conclave which would determine whether the Lord could set bones or whether He could not. *It is the duty of parents to* provide medical aid for their children. A child did not know anything about the tenets of the Peculiar People. While a child is of tender years and could not choose for itself, the law protects it. If the defendants neglected the duty which the law imposed upon them—the duty of calling in medical aid for the child—and death is thereby caused or accelerated, they are guilty of the charge made against them." The jury agreed that there was gross negligence, but could not agree that it accelerated death.

Regina *v.* Cook, Alb. L.J., vol. lviii, p. 232.

In another case, upon similar facts, the jury convicted, and the Court of Crown Cases Reserved affirmed the conviction; apparently, however, basing the affirmance upon the Prevention of Cruelty to Children Act (1894), 57 and 58 Vict. Ch., 41. The memorandum of decision is as follows: "A parent is guilty of manslaughter if, in consequence of his wilful refusal to provide medical aid for his child, the child dies, whatever may be the parent's motive. It is a doctrine of a religious sect, calling themselves ' The Peculiar People,' that it is sinful to administer drugs to the sick or to employ a physician. A member of the sect refused to supply medicine to his sick child, or to allow it to be attended by a medical man, and in consequence of the want of medical aid the child died.

"**Held**, that the parent was rightly convicted of manslaughter."

Regina *v.* Senior (decided Dec. 10th), *Law Times*, Dec. 17, 1898.

(Although this last case seems to be decided under the Prevention of Cruelty to Children Act, that statute does not expressly require that medical aid shall be furnished to children. See **Medical Record,** Jan. 21, 1899, p. 110. As bearing upon the excusability of parents who neglect ordinary medical safeguards for their children on account of conscientious motives, it may be noticed that the new English Vaccination Act relieves from penalties imposed for not vaccinating children, parents who satisfactorily prove to a magistrate or two justices their conscientious belief that vaccination is prejudicial to a child's health. See *Law Journal,* Oct. 1, 1898.)

Taxation—MEDICAL SOCIETY NOT EXEMPT AS BEING A CHARITABLE OR EDUCATIONAL BODY. — A medical society, organized under the New York statutes, Ch. 94, Ll. 1813, which maintains a medical library open to the public, furnishes rooms for the meeting of medical and charitable societies, and has established an organization for mental improvement and for certain educational and charitable purposes, but does not allege organization exclusively to carry out those purposes, or claim that its purpose is to improve morals, or of a religious, missionary, hospital, patriotic, historical, or cemetery nature, is not exempt from payment of taxes under Ch. 498, Ll. 1893.

> People ex rel. Med. Soc. Kings Co. *v.* Neff, et al., 34 App. Div., 83.

Sanctity of the Person—AUTOPSY (Ham., p. 632).—An action lies by a father to recover damages for an unauthorized autopsy upon his child.

> Burney *v.* Children's Hospital, 47 N.E., 401 (Mass., June, 1897). *Cf.* Larson *v.* Chase, 47 Minn., 307.

A wife has a similar action for unauthorized dissection of husband.

> Foley *v.* Phelps, 1 App. Div., 551. New York L.J., July 21, 1897, editorial.

And an insurance company cannot as matter of right hold an autopsy on the body of the insured.

> Wehle *v.* U. S. Mut. Accident Ass'n., 11 Misc., 36; 153 N.Y., 116.

Pharmacy — UNLAWFUL SALE BY EMPLOYEE—WHAT ARE RURAL DISTRICTS IN THE MEANING OF THE LAW.—Under the New York statute, where it appears that the sale of medicine in the shop of a person not a licensed pharmacist was made not by defendant personally, but by his servant and against the express orders of defendant, given in good faith and expectation that they would be obeyed—

Held, that an action for penalty would not lie against the employer, proof of such disobedience by a servant being a defence thereto.

Held, also, that the exemption in the statute in favor of retailers of usual domestic remedies in " rural districts," does not apply to the case of a dealer in a village of twelve thousand inhabitants, such rural districts being "small villages and country districts having no store where pharmacy is practised."

> Westchester Co. *v.* Dressner, 23 App. Div., 215; 48 N.Y.S., 953.

Assault by Administration of Drugs. — B., a druggist, knowingly put up for A. croton oil, to be administered in candy to C. as a practical joke.

Held, in an action for assault by C., that B. was liable for

any injuries sustained by plaintiff; and that it was not necessary that the dose should have been poisonous or deadly, it
being sufficient if it were unusual and liable to cause injury.

State *v.* Monroe, 28 S.E., 547 (N. C.).

Murder—EVIDENCE RELEVANT TO THE CHARGE.—The following case is of curious interest, in view of several *causes
célèbres* lately growing out of murders by medical students.

A. was indicted for murder. The State contended that the
body of the murdered man had been carried after death in a
buggy and in a sitting posture.

Held, that on this theory it was proper to show in evidence
that A., being present at the coroner's inquest, in talking of
the killing and his own lack of fear in presence of a corpse,
said, by way of illustration, that when the body of an old man
was turned over to the students when he was at the medical
school, they tied its hands and feet together, set it in a buggy,
strapped it to the seat, and put a hat on its head, with the
result that every one thought it was a living man.

People *v.* Schwartz, 76 N.W., 491.

This recalls the testimony in the case of Carlyle Harris, to
the effect that before his wife's murder by a morphine capsule,
he had been overheard saying to one of his paramours that she
ought to marry a rich old man, and he would give him a pill.

X-rays. See *supra*, under "Evidence."

A BRIEF

FOR THE PROSECUTIONS OF UNLICENSED PRACTITIONERS OF MEDICINE, DENTISTRY, OR PHARMACY.

I. Violations.

What are violations of statutes regulating the occupations referred to, must necessarily depend in each jurisdiction upon the terms of the State law, and for reasons already given the statutes of the different States are not here published.

The English Medical Act, which aims to prevent the false assumption of medical titles, does not prohibit the practice of medicine by unlicensed persons, but provides a system of medical registration whereunder registered practitioners have privileges not shared by the unregistered, and the latter are subjected to penalties if they pretend to be registered. The Dental Act is of like nature. But one who practises as an apothecary, without license, is liable to a penalty under the Apothecaries Act, and so is one who, without license, keeps a shop to sell poisons in violation of the Pharmaceutical Act.

In most of the United States, any person practising medicine, dentistry, or pharmacy without license is punishable civilly by a penalty, or criminally as a misdemeanant.

The New York act regulating the practice of dentistry, being more minute in its provisions than even the Medical Act, may serve as a sufficient illustration of American legislation of this nature.*

---

* In New York the practice of Medicine, Dentistry, and Pharmacy is now regulated by the Public Health Law, chapter xxv. o f the General Laws, enacted by chapter 661 of the Laws of 1893.

THE MEDICAL LAW consists of sections 140 to 153 inclusive as amended by chapters 398 and 636, Laws of 1895, and chapter 111, Laws of 1896.

THE DENTAL LAW consists of sections 160 to 164 inclusive as amended

That act, which consists of Sections 160–164 of Chapter xxv. of the General Laws, as amended, creates a State board to examine candidates for license, who must have received dental instruction, attested by a diploma or license, and also a certain preliminary general education. Candidates are presented to the board, and, if successful before it, are licensed by the regents of the university of the State; and licentiates, before engaging in practice, must register their licenses with the clerk of the county wherein they intend to practise, and upon moving to another county or engaging in practice therein must register in the latter county also.

II. Penalties.

The act, by Section 164, entitled " Penalties," punishes as a misdemeanor dental practice, or the holding out of himself as a práctising dentist to the public, by any person not licensed and registered in the office of the clerk of the county pursuant to the statute. This misdemeanor, the one most frequently prosecuted, is punished by a fine of not less than $50 for the first offence, and for any subsequent offence by a fine of not less than $100, or imprisonment for not less than two months, or by both such fine and imprisonment.

The other misdemeanors created by the act involve in their essence, fraud and false pretense, and are punishable by a fine of not less than $500, the usual maximum fine for a misdemeanor, or by imprisonment of not less than six months, or by both fine and imprisonment. They are enumerated in subdivision (*b*) of said section, and consist in purchasing or selling diplomas, certificates, or transcripts contemplated by the act, fraudulent alterations thereof, fraudulent use thereof, the practice of dentistry under false or assumed names, and the false assumption of a dental or medical degree.

The purchase and sale of said documents is not uncommon, and the assumption of false names and degrees, especially by persons practising in so-called dental " parlors," is of frequent occurrence.

by chapter 626, Laws of 1895, chapter 297, Laws of 1896, and chapter 355, Laws of 1898.

THE PHARMACY LAW consists of sections 180 to 190 inclusive as amended by chapter 896, Laws of 1895, chapter 253, Laws of 1896, and chapter 297, Laws of 1897.

Conviction of felony works a forfeiture of license, and any person who, after such unreversed conviction, shall practise dentistry, is subject to all the penalties attaching to unlicensed practice (Section 162, subdivision entitled "Revocation of licenses ")

The only felony created by the act is false swearing in the affidavit or examination required of candidates for license, which is made perjury.

III. Constitutionality of the Law.

Such laws are constitutional if they operate upon all in the same manner and degree; and a statute forbidding any one to practise these professions after a certain date, unless he shall first pass an examination before a State board of examiners and register his name and license with a county clerk, is a proper exercise of the police power, does not create a monopoly, does not abolish vested rights or take property without due process of law, even though it affect persons already in practice, and does not necessarily create a "privileged class," although it exempt from its operation general classes, *e.g.*, persons already practising, and medical staffs of the army and navy, marine, and other hospitals.

(1) Medical Laws.

Dent *v.* West Va., 129 U. S., 114.
Hawker *v.* New York, 170 U. S., 189.
Richardson *v.* State (Ark.), 2 S.W., 187.
Ex parte McNulty (Cal.), 19 Pac., 237.
Brown *v.* People (Colo.), 17 Pac., 104.
Harding *v.* People (Colo.), 15 Pac., 727.
Williams *v.* People (Ill.), 11 N.E., 881.
Eastman *v.* State (Ind.), 10 N.E., 99.
Orr *v.* Meek (Ind.), 11 N.E., 787.
State *v.* Green (Ind.), 14 N.E., 352.
State *v.* Webster (Ind.), 50 N.E., 750.
Commonwealth *v.* Rice (Ky.), 20 S.W., 703.
Driscoll *v.* Commonwealth (Ky.), 20 S.W., 431.
Hewitt *v.* Charier (Mass.), 33 Mass. (16 Pick.), 353.
People *v.* Phippin (Mich.), 70 Mich., 6; 37 N.W., 888.

State *v*. Board (Minn.), 26 N.W., 123.
State *v*. Fleischer (Minn.), 42 N.W., 696.
State *v*. Hathaway (Mo.), 21 S.W., 1081.
Gee Wo *v*. State 46 (Nebr.), 54 N.W., 513 (overruled by O'Connor *v*. State, 46 Nebr., 157; 64 N.W., 719).
Re Roe Chung (N. M.), 49 Pac., 952.
People *v*. Hawker, 14 App. Div., 188; rev'd 152 N. Y., 234.
State *v*. Call (N. C.), 121 N. C., 643; 28 S.E., 517.
France *v*. State (Ohio), 57 Ohio St., 1.
State *v*. Morrill (Ohio), 7 Ohio Dec., 52.
State *v*. Ottman (Ohio), 6 Ohio Dec., 195.
State *v*. Randolph (Oreg.), 31 Pac., 201.
Commonwealth *v*. Wilson (Pa.), 19 Pa. Co. Ct. R., 521.
Dowdell *v*. McBride (Tex.), 45 S.W., 397.
Kennedy *v*. Schultz (Tex.), 25 S.W., 667.
Fox *v*. Territory (Wash. T.), 5 Pac., 603.

(2) Dental Laws.

Gosnell *v*. State (Ark.), 12 S.W., 392.
State *v*. Creditor (Kans.), 24 Pac., 346.
State *v*. Vandersluis (Minn.), 42 Minn., 129.
Commonwealth *v*. Gibson (Pa.), 7 Pa. Dist. R., 386.

(3) Pharmacy Laws.

People *v*. Moorman (Mich.), 49 N.W., 263.
State *v*. Forcier (N. H.), 17 Atl., 577.
People *v*. Rontey, 4 N. Y. Sup., 235; Af'd 117 N. Y., 624.
State *v*. Heinemann (Wis.), 80 Wis., 253; 49 N.W., 818.
In a few cases such laws have been held to be unconstitutional, as creating privileged classes or taking property without due process of law.
State *v*. Pennoyer, 65 N. H., 113 (physicians).
State *v*. Hinman, 65 N. H., 103; 18 Atl., 194 (dentists).
Rutter *v*. Rodgers, 8 Pa. Co. Ct. R., 451.
Cf. the dissenting opinions in
People *v*. Phippin (Mich.), 70 Mich., 6; 37 N.W., 888.

Ex parte Spinney (Nev.), 10 Nev., 323.
Hawker *v.* New York and People *v.* Hawker (*supra*).

In Hawker's case it was held the New York statute forbidding any one to practise medicine after conviction of felony was not *ex post facto*, in its application to persons so convicted prior to its passage, but provided only a test of character, not an additional punishment.

The course of decision in the case was curious. Apparently the record did not show that defendant was ever lawfully entitled to practise medicine, but only that, having been convicted of felony prior to the enactment of the law, he practised medicine thereafter contrary to the statute. The trial judge held the statute to be valid, apparently *pro forma*. Four out of five judges of the appellate division reversed the judgment, and, assuming the defendant to have been lawfully practising prior to his conviction, held the statute to be *ex post facto* in so far as it operated to punish an old offence by an additional penalty, to wit, the deprivation of license. Five judges of the court of appeals agreed to reverse the appellate division and affirm judgment of conviction upon the ground that the record did not show that defendant ever was entitled to practise. One of them concurred solely because the record did not show that defendant ever was a physician; but the other four judges seem also to have considered that even if defendant had possessed such a right, the conviction might still have been valid. Two judges dissented. In the Supreme Court of the United States, upon a reargument, the judgment of the court of appeals and the conviction were affirmed, without regard, apparently, to the failure of the record to show that defendant ever had a medical license, and expressly upon the ground that the law, even in so far as retroactive, was not *ex post facto*, but was constitutional; three judges dissenting. It would seem, therefore, that the judges of all courts, assuming defendant to have been lawfully entitled to practise when the law was enacted, were evenly divided upon the question of the statute's constitutionality in so far as it is retroactive. (See *Medical Record*, July 24, 1897, vol. lii., p. 114.)

No doubt at all was expressed as to the validity of the law in its prospective operation.

Cf. France *v.* State (Ohio), 57 Ohio St., 1; 47 N.E., 1041.

IV. The Indictment or Complaint.

It is sufficient to charge the offence in the language of the
statute without alleging the particular acts constituting the
practice.   But the facts rendering the practice unlawful—*e.g.*,
that the accused was not at the time of practice licensed or
registered—must be alleged.

> Eastman *v.* State (Ind.), 10 N.E., 87.
> People *v.* Phippin (Mich.), 70 Mich., 6; 37 N.W., 888.
> Sheldon *v.* Clark (N. Y.), 1 Johns., 513.
> People *v.* Dorthy (N. Y.), 20 App. Div., 308.
> County of Steuben *v.* Wood (N. Y.), 24 App. Div., 442.
> State *v.* Morrill (Ohio), 7 Ohio Dec., 52.
> State *v.* Pirlot (R. I.), 38 Atl., 656.

See also—

> Cook *v.* People (Ill.), 17 N. E., 849 (pharmacist).
> Dee *v.* State (Miss.), 9 So., 356 (physicians).
> Denton *v.* State (Nebr.), 32 N.W., 222.
> State *v.* Call (N. C.), 121 N. C., 643; 28 S.E., 517.
> State *v.* Ragland (W. Va.), 7 S.E., 788 (itinerants).
> Whitlock *v.* Commonwealth (Va.), 15 S.E., 893.

If the statute enumerates what acts shall constitute the practice of medicine, the commission of some or all of those acts
must be pleaded.

> State *v.* Carey (Wash.), 4 Wash St., 788; 30 Pac., 729.
> *Cf.* State *v.* Hathaway (Mo.), 21 S.W., 1081.
> O'Connor *v.* State (Nebr.), 46 Nebr., 157; 64 N.W., 719.

An indictment is defective that charges practice without license from a different board than the one named by the statute.

> Derrick *v.* State (Tex.), 28 S.W., 818.

And see also—

> State *v.* Fussell, 46 Ark., 65.
> State *v.* Hale (Mo.), 15 Mo., 606.
> State *v.* Roberts, 33 Mo. App., 524.
> State *v.* Goldman (Tex.), 44 Tex., 104.

It is not necessary to negative the exemptions of the statute unless they are in the enacting clause.   That the accused is one of a
class exempted from the statute's operation is matter of defence.

> Harding *v.* People (Colo.), 15 Pac., 727.
> People *v.* Phippin (Mich.), 70 Mich., 6; *supra*.

State *v.* Smith (Mo.), 1 Mo. Ap. R., 129.
County of Steuben *v.* Wood (N. Y.), 24 App. Div., 442;
  48 Supl., 471.
State *v.* Call (N. C.), 121 N. C., 643; 28 S.E., 517.
State *v.* Morril (Ohio), 7 Ohio Dec., 52.
Krownestrot *v.* State (Ohio), 8 Ohio Dec., 119.
Hale *v.* State (Ohio), 51 N.E., 154.
State *v.* Barker (Vt.), 18 Vt., 195.

When the statute authorized a physician to register upon affidavit that he had been in practice for ten years prior to 1874, a complaint alleging that defendant had registered upon affidavits that he had been in practice for twelve years prior to 1889 was held to charge sufficiently the offence.

Driscoll *v.* Commonwealth (Ky.), 20 S.W., 431.
Cf. Rice *v.* Commonwealth (Ky.), 20 S.W., 703.

To allege that defendant is not within any of the excepted classes is a sufficient negative.

State *v.* Hathaway (Mo.), 21 S.W., 1081.

It is not necessary to allege criminal intent or receipt of fees unless the statute makes such an intent or compensation an element of the offence.

Harding *v.* People (Colo.), 15 Pac., 727.
Eastman *v.* State (Ind.), 10 N.E., 99.
Whitlock *v.* Commonwealth (Va.), 15 S.E., 893.
Bishop's Crim. Proc., sec. 523.

Where unlicensed itinerant venders of drugs are forbidden to "profess to treat disease" it is not necessary to allege that drugs were sold or used.

State *v.* Blair (Iowa), 60 N.W., 486.

Where the offence may be committed in several ways, to allege various ways—*e.g.*, a holding out by printing, writing, and other methods—is not to charge two offences.

State *v.* Blair (Iowa), 60 N.W., 486.

V. The Usual Issues in Such Prosecutions.

The issues in these prosecutions are:

(1) Did the defendant practise medicine or dentistry, or act as a pharmacist within the county?

(2) If so, was he licensed or registered according to law?

(3) If not, was he within any exemption of the statute?

VI. Order and Burden of Proof.

The prosecution needs only to prove that defendant practised or held himself out as practising medicine or dentistry, or conducted a pharmacy, as alleged in the indictment. It may then rest.

The burden of proof then shifts to defendant, who must either—

(*a*) Rebut the prosecutor's proof by testimony that he did not do the acts testified to by the people's witnesses; or

(*b*) Show that he is licensed and registered as the statute requires; or

(*c*) Show that he is within the exemptions, if any, of the statute.

If the prosecution had to prove that defendant was not licensed or registered, it would be called on to prove a negative, and this might be impossible, especially in jurisdictions where any diploma is a license; on the other hand, whether defendant is licensed or registered is a fact peculiarly within his knowledge and easy for him to prove; the question is not one, therefore, of merits, but only of order of proof.

Lawson's "Presumptions of Evidence," p. 20.

Apothecaries Co. *v*. Bentley, 1 C. & P., 538.

Benham *v*. State (Ind.), 18 N.W., 454; 116 Ind., 112.

People *v*. Nyce (N. Y.), 34 Hun, 298.

People *v*. Fulda (N. Y.), 52 Hun, 65.

People *v*. Rontey (N. Y.), 4 N. Y. Supl., 235; 117 N. Y., 624.

Raynor *v*. State (Wis.), 62 Wis., 289; 22 N.W., 430.

Second Offence.

Where defendant is charged with a second offence his previous conviction must be proved if alleged in the indictment.

People *v*. Reilly (N. Y.), 25 Misc., 45.

And the commission of the first offence may be proved against the objection of defendant, and although he admits the fact.

People *v*. Sickles (N. Y.), 26 App. Div., 470; Af'd 156 N. Y., 541; N.Y.L.J., Oct. 28, 1898, 53 Supl., 288.

VII. The Prosecution's Case.

The prosecution being only bound to make proof as above, the questions arise:

What is practice of medicine or holding out?

What is practice of dentistry or holding out?

What is the conduct of a pharmacy?

The answers to these questions must depend in each instance upon the phrasing of the statute under which the defendant is prosecuted and the peculiar circumstances of the particular case.

The General Rule.

The offence may be established *prima facie* by proof of a single case of practice, together with any circumstances showing intent.

Sheldon *v*. Clark (N. Y.), 1 Johns., 513.

Thompson *v*. Staats (N. Y.), 15 Wend, 395.

Antle *v*. State, 6 Tex. App., 202.

Ellison *v*. State (Tex.), 6 Tex. App., 249.

That defendant displayed a physician's sign or otherwise solicited medical practice is evidence of holding out.

State *v.* Van Doran (N. C.), 109 N. C., 864.

In What Practice Consists.

The practice of medicine has been said, in the absence of statutory definition, to consist: First, in judging the nature, character, and symptoms of the disease; second, in determining the proper remedy for the disease; third, in giving or prescribing the application of the remedy to the disease.

Underwood *v*. Scott (Kans.), 43 Kans., 714.

And it has been also said that the test of medical practice is the administration of medicine or the use of instruments; by which criterion the giving of massage is not practice of medicine,

Smith *v*. Lane 632 (N. Y.); 24 Hun, 632

nor is a clairvoyant's treatment,

6

Wood *v.* Kelly (Mass.), 62 Mass. (8 Cush.), 406.
But these broad definitions cannot be accepted without lim-
itation.   The physician who directs nature without the use of
drugs or instruments often succeeds best.   And the ignorant
impostor who pretends to cure by other than customary methods
is often one of the worst offenders against the statute.   And
accordingly, contrary to the doctrine of those cases, it has been
held,

in Hewitt *v.* Charrier (Mass.), 16 Pick., 353,
that a bonesetter was a medical practitioner;

in Bibber *v.* Simpson (Me.), 59 Me., 181,
that a clairvoyant was a medical practitioner;

in People *v.* Phippin (Mich.), 70 Mich., 6 (*supra*),
that one styling himself Dr. Phippin, magnetic healer, who
treated the sick as a magnetic healer, and signed a death certificate as Dr. Phippin, Magnetic Healer, was rightly convicted
of practising medicine unlawfully;   .

in Benham *v.* State (Ind.), 116 Ind., 112; 18 N.W., 454,
that one advertising as Dr. Benham, and undertaking to cure
the opium habit, practised medicine;

and in Hardings *v.* People (Colo.), 15 Pac., 727,
Davidson *v.* Bohlman (Mo.), 37 Mo. Ap., 576,
Nelson *v.* Harrington (Wis.), 72 Wis., 591; 40 N.W.,
228,
that attempting to cure the sick by electrical treatment was
practice of medicine.

WHETHER THE ACTS COMPLAINED OF CONSTITUTE PRACTICE OF
    MEDICINE MUST LARGELY DEPEND UPON THE DEFINITION
        OF SUCH PRACTICE, IF ANY, CONTAINED IN THE STATUTE.

Thus under the Ohio statute defining a medical practitioner
to be one who for a fee prescribes or "recommends" any drug,
medicine, "or other agency" for the treatment of any bodily
injury or disease, it was held that the general words were so
limited by the special words that an "osteopath" was not such
a practitioner within the meaning of the statute.

Eastman *v.* State (Ohio), 6 Ohio Dec., 296.
But under the Illinois statute defining such practitioners as
persons who "treat, operate on, or prescribe for any physical
ailment of another," an "osteopath" was held to be liable to
the penalty imposed upon those unlawfully practising medicine.

Eastman *v.* People (Ill.), 71 Ill. App., 236.
So also a midwife—
People *v.* Arendt (Ill.), 60 Ill. App., 89.
Cf. Luck *v.* Ripon (Wis.), 52 Wis., 196.
In Nebraska the performances of a Christian Scientist were held to be practice of medicine within the definition of the statute,
State *v.* Buswell (Nebr.) 40 Neb., 158;
while the contrary was held in Rhode Island,
State *v.* Mylod (R. I.), 40 Atl., 753.
Under a statute of Maine allowing recovery of compensation for medical services by any one possessed of a certificate of good moral character from town officers, it was held that a Christian Scientist having such a certificate might sue for fees. The case, however, is no authority upon the question, what constitutes medical practice.

A farmer attempting to cure cancer by a recipe and holding himself out as a cancer doctor was held to have practised medicine.
Musser's Executors *v.* Chase, 29 Ohio St., 577.
Where the statute permits one in practice at the date of its enactment to continue in practice, such a person is a "physician," although not graduated as a doctor.
Harrison *v.* State (Ala.), 15 So., 563.
A shoemaker also engaging in medical practice is not apparently a reputable and honorable practitioner of medicine in Rhode Island.
Paquin *v.* St. Bd. of Health (R. I.), 33 Atl., 870.
A license to practise medicine authorizes the holder to practise surgery.
Clinton Co. *v.* Ramsey (Ill.), 20 Ill. App., 577.
Wetherell *v.* Marion Co., 28 Iowa, 22.
Stewart *v.* Raab (Minn.), 56 N.W., 256.
A homœopathist or eclectic is a medical practitioner, and one medical school is not favored at the expense of another.
Force *v.* Gregory (Conn.), 27 Atl., 1116.
Patten *v.* Wiggin, 51 Me., 594.
Corsi *v.* Maretzek (N. Y.), 4 E. D. Smith, 1.
White *v.* Carroll (N. Y.), 42 N. Y., 161.
Raynor *v.* State (Wis.), 62 Wis., 289.
Cf. Dowdell *v.* McBride (Tex.), 45 S.W., 397.

Cf. State *v.* Mylod (R. I.), 40 Atl., 753.

Defendant's admissions upon another trial are admissible against him to prove practice, although his self-serving statement may be excluded.

Suffolk Co. *v.* Shaw, 21 App. Div., 146.

But one cannot under guise of selling patent medicines or drugs prescribe and advise as a physician.

Underwood *v.* Scott (Kans.), 43 Kans., 714; 23 Pac., 942.

Alcott *v.* Barber (N. Y.), 1 Wend., 526.

Thompson *v.* Staats (N. Y.), 15 Wend., 395.

Smith *v.* Tracy (N. Y.), 2 Hall, 465.

(The above principle is applicable to the cases of druggists, chemists, apothecaries, etc., who undertake to make diagnosis and give advice.)

Matthei *v.* Wooley (Ill.), 69 Ill. App., 634.

One who practises under the guise of being the pupil or assistant of a physician may be within the purview of the statute.

Richardson *v.* State (Ark.), 2 S.W., 188.

State *v.* Paul (Nebr.), 76 N.W., 861.

But it has been held that one called doctor by his neighbors, and accustomed to gather herbs and advise his sick friends without fee, was held not to be a medical practitioner.

Nelson *v.* State (Ala.), 12 So., 421.

And that a farrier occasionally prescribing for human beings is not an apothecary.

Apothecaries' Co. *v.* Warburton, 3 Barn & Ad., 40.

Cf. Steed *v.* Henley, 1 C. & P., 574.

So, too, it has been said that to advise and prescribe for several persons in one day does not constitute several offences, the gist of practice being customary action.

Apothecaries' Co. *v.* Jones, 1 Q. B. D., (1893), 89.

Cf. Greenfield *v.* Gilman (N. Y.), 140 N. Y., 168.

Cf. Pedgrift *v.* Chevallier, 8 C. B. N. S., 240.

And upon the whole topic, see—

"A System of Legal Medicine," by Allan McLane Hamilton, and others (vol. i., pp. 602–604).

Dentistry.

The same general principles that apply to medical practice afford the test of what is dental practice.

Evidence that defendant leased rooms with the avowed purpose of practising dentistry, performed dental work for several persons, and worked at the bench, establishes the practice.

Ferner *v.* State (Ind.), 51 N.E., 360.
See as to the status and definition of dentistry—
Maxon *v.* Perrott (Mich.), 17 Mich., 332.
People *v.* De France (Mich.), 104 Mich., 503.
State *ex rel.* Flickenger *v.* Fisher (Mo.), 119 Mo., 353.
Whitcomb *v.* Reed (Miss.), 31 Miss., 567.
Lee *v.* Griffin, 30 L. J. Q. B., 252.
"*Code de Chirurgien-Dentiste,*" p. 88.
Hamilton's "System of Legal Medicine," vol. i., p. 641.
See also the statute in each State.

Pharmacists and Druggists.

See the Hypophosphite & Borax Cases (Minn.), 41 Minn., 74; 42 N.W., 781.

It is a violation of the Illinois Act for the proprietor of a drug-shop to instruct his boy to sell anything but poison, leaving the lad to judge what are poisons.

Haas *v.* People (Ill.), 27 Ill. App., 416.
Cf. Pharmaceutical Soc. *v.* Wheeldon (Eng.), 24 Q. B. Div., 683.

Quinine is not a "domestic remedy" within the Illinois act, and its sale is evidence of unlawful practice of pharmacy.

Cook *v.* People (Ill.), 17 N.E., 849.

Sale of paregoric and quinine pills in the original packages, by an unlicensed clerk in a department store, is a violation of the pharmacy act.

People *v.* Abraham (N. Y.), 16 App. Div., 58.

A physician who sells drugs which he has not prescribed may come within the purview of the statute.

State *v.* Jones (Oreg.), 22 Pac., 840.
Cf. Suffolk Co. *v.* Shaw (N. Y.), 21 App. Div., 146.

Cf. People *v.* Rontey (N. Y.), 4 N. Y. Supl., 235 (*supra*).
And see the cases cited below under " Defences."
And see further as to the relations of physicians, surgeons,
and apothecaries among themselves—

Allison *v.* Hayden, 4 Bing., 617.

Apothecaries Co. *v.* Lotinga, 2 Mo. & R., 495.

VIII. The Case of Defendant.

Where defendant has not successfully demurred to the indictment, and the prosecution, by proving practice, has shifted
the burden of proof, the former must, in order to disprove the
charge, establish, as aforesaid, either:

(1) That the prosecution's testimony is not true beyond
reasonable doubt; or

(2) That he has a right to perform the acts proved because—

(*a*) He was licensed and registered as required by the
statute; or

(*b*) Was within one of the classes exempted from the operation of the statute.

I. As to Disproof of the Prosecution's Case.

Where the testimony against the accused is that of his actual
patients, there is little room for reasonable doubt in the minds
of intelligent and conscientious jurors; especially if the patients testify reluctantly and under subpœna.   But sometimes,
especially in rural districts and small towns, and where the
witnesses are detectives or persons hostile to the accused, both
grand and petit jurors, swayed by personal predilections, decide
the issues in violation of their oaths, not upon the testimony,
but upon their sentiments or information extraneous to the
case.   Thus in Herkimer county a grand jury thrice refused,
upon overwhelming evidence and in disregard of explicit instructions, to indict a notorious violator of the dental law, who
had even gone to the extent of perjuring himself in order to
qualify as an expert in a malpractice case; and their breach
of duty, which was largely due to the fact that the accused
had been reported by an unpopular rival, was applauded by
the local press.

So in a Warsaw case the grand jury refused to indict an unregistered native of the town, but actually did indict his unregistered rival practitioner who had recently come into the neighborhood.

But although the prosecution's case may in rare instances be overcome by such improper appeals to prejudice, especially if it rests solely on the testimony of detectives or agents who have submitted to defendant's practice for the purpose of testifying against him; nevertheless, testimony of such agents is competent, and if believed sufficient, to sustain a verdict of guilty.

People *v.* Noelke, 1 N. Y. Cr. R., 252, at p. 264; af'd 94 N. Y., 197.

II. Proof of License.

(A) State License.

Where the license is conferred by the State the certificate may readily be produced and proved. In some jurisdictions a transcript of the record is expressly made *prima facie* evidence of its facts.

(B) Diplomas.

Where the license required is a diploma, the accused may have more difficulty in establishing his defence, especially if his diploma is from a school without the jurisdiction and the court insists on strict rules of evidence; in such a case defendant must show the authority of the institution from which he holds the diploma to confer the degree, and also the regularity of the document, and, *semble*, that the bearer has complied with preliminary requirements.

Moises *v.* Thornton, 8 T. R., 303.
Chadwick *v.* Bunning, 2 C. & P., 106.
Collins *v.* Carnegie, 1 A. & E., 695.
Andrews *v.* Styrap, 26 L. T. R., 704.
Hill *v.* Boddie (Ala.), 2 Stew. & P., 56.
Hunter *v.* Blount (Ga.), 27 Ga., 76.

In practice, the rigor of the strict rule is often or generally relaxed.

Walmisley *v.* Abbott, 1 C. & P., 309, 495.
Finch *v.* Gridley's Executors (N. Y.), 25 Wend., 469.
Wendel *v.* State (Wis.), 62 Wis., 300.

(C) REGISTRATION.

(1) Where the accused is entitled to register, and has done all required of him by the statute to that end, it would seem that he will not be chargeable with failure to register due to the fault of the registering officer—*e.g.*, where pursuant to the law he mails his credentials to a county clerk, who fails to make the proper registry.

Parish *v.* Foss, 75 Ga., 439.
Pettit *v.* State (Tex.), 28 Tex. App., 240; 14 S.W., 127.
Cf. Carberry *v.* People, 39 Ill. App., 506.
Cf. Hamilton, "System of Legal Medicine," p. 601.

(2) But if a State board refuse to grant a license to A, he cannot show by way of defence to a prosecution for unlawful practice that such refusal was wrongful. If the board deny his rights, the remedy is by mandamus.

Kowenstrot *v.* State (Ohio), 8 Ohio Dec., 119.

(3) The fact that defendant is registered in one county of the State is not ordinarily a defence to a charge of practising without registration in another.

Orr *v.* Meek (Ind.), 111 Ind., 40; 11 N.E., 787.
Hayes *v.* Webster (N. Y.), N. Y. Daily Reg., Jan. 26, 1884.
Ege *v.* Commonwealth (Pa.), 8 Cent., 539; 9 Atl., 471.
Hilliard *v.* State (Tex.), 7 Tex. App., 69.

The case of

Martino *v.* Kirk, 55 Hun, 474,

which is cited to the contrary, is ill-considered and scarcely authority. It seems to have been decided under the law of 1880, which had been repealed by the law of 1887; and the question was presented collaterally in a civil action to recover compensation for services.

(D) Exemptions.

(*1*) *Fees.*

Where the statute forbids only practice for compensation it is a defence that the services proven were rendered gratuitously.
Nelson *v.* State (Ala.), 12 So., 421.
But actual payment need not be shown if the testimony is such that the jury may properly infer from it an intent by the accused to receive compensation,
State *v.* Hale (Mo.), 15 Mo., 606;
or if the statute only forbids the practice in general terms without mention of compensation,
Eastman *v.* State (Ind.), 10 N.E., 99.

(*2*) *Emergencies.*

If the statute exempt from its operation persons rendering aid in emergency, it must be shown that the attendance of a licentiate was not obtainable. The fact that licensed physicians have failed to effect a cure is not an emergency justifying practice by an unlicensed person.
People *v.* Lee Wah (Cal.), 71 Cal., 80; 11 Pac., 851.

(*3*) *Assistants.*

(*a*) When the statute permits students to assist preceptors for purposes of clinical instruction or otherwise, a student cannot under the pretence of assisting perform independent acts of practice out of the presence of his preceptor.
Richardson *v.* State (Ark.), 2 S.W., 188.
State *v.* Paul (Nebr.), 76 N.W., 861.
(*b*) So the unregistered assistant of a pharmacist may not do any acts forbidden to the unlicensed.
Pharmaceutical Society *v.* Wheeldon, 24 Q. B. Div., 683.
(*c*) But if in the principal's absence a servant sell contrary to orders, the principal will not be liable.
Westchester Co. *v.* Dressner (N. Y.), 23 App. Div., 215;
48 N. Y. Supl., 953.
(*d*) So under the New York dental statute exempting the stu-

dent of a licentiate "assisting his preceptor in dental operations while in the presence and under the personal supervision
of the instructor," it has been held in a number of unreported
cases that such a student cannot perform independent operations or carry on a branch of the business, but must in fact
"assist" the preceptor.

(4) Sale of Drugs in Rural Communities.

Where the statute exempts from provisions of pharmacy acts,
traders in rural communities, it has been held that a town of
twelve thousand inhabitants is not a rural community.

Westchester Co. v. Dressner (N. Y.), 23 App. Div., 215;
48 N. Y. Supl., 953.

The principles of the foregoing cases apply to exemptions
generally.

MANSLAUGHTER, CHRISTIAN SCIENCE, AND THE LAW.

By WILLIAM A. PURRINGTON.

THE recent death of Mr. Harold Frederic under the treatment of a Christian scientist, and the latter's indictment by an English jury, have renewed the discussion by professional and lay journals of what is and what should be the bearing of the law upon such cases.

The New York *Times*, of which he was correspondent, writes editorially of "Faith-Cure Murders"; *The Sun*, of "Manslaughter by Christian Science." The current law journals comment upon the case. Unfortunately, such instances are neither modern nor rare.

Coincidently with Mr. Frederic's death from pneumonia in England, the newspapers also report the deaths of Messrs. Kershaw in Tacoma, and McDowell in Cincinnati, and Mrs. Brown, of Washington; the first of pneumonia, the second of typhoid fever, the last of an unnamed malady—all the diseases being complicated with Christian Science. It is only Frederic's prominence as a journalist and fiction writer that brings his case nearer home to the multitude.

The ordinary quack is content to lay claim to some special skill or knowledge in the use of natural methods or remedies. Thus in February, 1806, one John M. Crous induced the same Legislature of New York that in the following April chartered the existing county and State medical societies, to authorize by special act the purchase for $1,000 and publication in the State papers of his "perfect and infallible remedy and cure for hydrophobia or canine madness." And a wonderful remedy it was.*

---

* Here is the prescription, and it certainly seems adequate to put an end to hydrophobia or any other malady :

In the following year an act (ch. 104, Ll. 1807) passed prohibiting unlicensed practice of medicine; with the proviso,
however, that it should not be construed to debar any one from
using, or applying for the benefit of the sick, roots or herbs
the growth or product of the United States. This exception
favored at once the principle of protection to the industry of
home herbs and the teachings of the Thomsonian or botanic
school of medicine, founded upon the simple, obvious theory
that mineral remedies are injurious because, their nature being
to remain in the earth, they tend to drag man down to the
grave; while herbs, having by nature an upward, skyward
thrust, tend, on the contrary, to the advancement of those
"whose midst" they penetrate.

This system, once as popular as Christian Science, furnished
the leading American case on manslaughter by medical malpractice, that of Commonwealth *v.* Thomson (6 Mass., 134).
It there appeared that Samuel Thomson, founder of the system,
undertook to cure "all fevers, whether black, gray, green, or

"First : Take one ounce of the jawbone of a dog, burned and pulverized, or pounded to fine dust.
"Secondly : Take the false tongue of a newly foaled colt ; let that be
also dried and pulverized ; and,
"Thirdly : Take one scruple of verdigris, which is raised on the surface of old copper by lying in the moist earth ; the coppers of George I.
or II. are the purest and best. Mix these ingredients together, and if the
person be an adult or full grown, take one common teaspoonful a day, and
so in proportion for a child according to its age. In one hour after take the
filings of the one-half a copper of the above kind, if to be had ; if not,
then a small increased quantity of any baser metal of the kind ; this to be
taken in a small quantity of water.
"The next morning, fasting (or before eating), repeat the same as
before. This, if complied with after the biting of a dog, and before the
symptoms of madness, will effectually prevent any appearance of disorder ;
but after the symptoms shall appear a physician must immediately be
applied to, to administer the following, viz. :
"Three drachms of the verdigris of the kind before mentioned, mixed
with half an ounce of calomel, to be taken at one dose. This quantity the
physician need not fear to administer, as the reaction of the venom will
then, diffuse through the whole system of the patient, neutralize consider-
ably the powerful quality of the medicine ; and,
"Secondly : If in four hours thereafter the patient is not completely
relieved, administer four grains of pure opium or one hundred and twenty
drops of liquid laudanum.
' N.B.—The patient must be careful to avoid the use of milk for several days after taking any of the foregoing medicine.
"JOHN M. CROUS."

yellow." His staple remedies were "coffee," so-called, "well my gristle," and "ram-cats." Being summoned on January 2d, 1809, to attend Ezra Lovett, ill of "a cold," he ordered a fire built, put Lovett's feet on a stove of hot coals, wrapped him in a blanket, and, with a powder given in water, "puked" him— to use the simple language of the day—violently thrice within half an hour, meantime administering copiously the warm "coffee." He then put Lovett to bed, and sweated and "puked" him pretty steadily for three days, the patient growing weaker and weaker, until, poor soul! he could puke no more. Then Thomson asked "how far down the medicine had got," and, Lovett indicating his chest, the quack said that the medicine "would soon get down and unscrew his navel." On the third day the patient "lost his mind and went into convulsions," which condition lasted until the eighth day, January 10th, when he died. The "coffee" proved to be a decoction of marshrosemary and the bark of the bayberry bush; the powder was Indian tobacco or Lobelia inflata. There was no evidence that defendant had killed any one else; on the contrary, there was testimony of benefit in one case from his treatment. The court, therefore, did not put him to his defence, but, ruling that the commonwealth had failed to make out a case even of manslaughter, charged the jury to this effect: Deceased, beyond reasonable doubt, lost his life by defendant's unskilful treatment. But there could be no murder, unless the prisoner was wilfully regardless of his social duty and determined on mischief, of which there was no proof; on the contrary, his intent was to cure. Neither could there be manslaughter; for, although defendant's ignorance was very apparent, nevertheless, if he honestly intended to cure, he could not be guilty of that crime on account of death unexpectedly ensuing from his treatment, unless he was engaged in an unlawful act; and there was no law in Massachusetts forbidding any man, honestly intending to cure, from prescribing for a sick man with the latter's consent. The court cited Lord Hale as authority for the proposition that, "if a physician, whether licensed or not, gives a person a potion, without any intent of doing him any bodily hurt, but with intent to cure or prevent a disease, and, contrary to the expectation of the physician, it kills him, he is not guilty of murder or manslaughter"; and, accordingly, laid down this law for the case:

"The death of a man, killed by voluntarily following a medical prescription, cannot be adjudged a felony in the party prescribing, unless he, however ignorant of medical science in general, had so much knowledge or probable information of the fatal tendency of the prescription that it may be reasonably presumed by the jury to be the effect of obstinate, wilful rashness, at the least, and not of an honest intention and expectation to cure."

The court further said that if the solicitor-general had proved, as he promised to do in his opening, that Thomson had killed others by his treatment, it would have been left to the jury to say whether on the whole evidence they would sustain the charge of manslaughter; which they might justly have done if they had found that defendant acted from "obstinate rashness and foolhardy presumption, although without intent to do Lovett bodily harm"; for it would not have been lawful for him again to administer a medicine of which he had such fatal experience. Upon this reasoning Thomson was acquitted; and his case having proved, as a precedent, a strong shield for manslaughtering charlatans, by establishing what has been called the humane American rule as contrasted with the strict rule of common law, it is well to state succinctly the reasons why he escaped conviction, viz.: (1) because there was no statute in Massachusetts prohibiting medical practice by the ignorant and unlicensed; (2) because there was no proof that Thomson (a) knew his treatment to be dangerous or (b) had any other intent than to cure in good faith.

In 1842 the question arose in New York, upon an application for a bill of discovery, in Marsh v. Davison (9 Paige, 580), whether it was slanderous to have said of complainant that he was guilty of malpractice as a cancer doctor and had killed a woman in Schoharie. Davison not being licensed to practice, the court held that—inasmuch as he might be guilty of manslaughter, for that reason, if the patient died under his treatment—the words might be slanderous.

It thus appears that—even accepting the benign rule of Thomson's case, which, as we shall see presently, was ill stated —wherever a statute makes the unlicensed practice of medicine a misdemeanor, if death result from the treatment of a non-licentiate he is guilty of manslaughter at least, no matter how honest his intent. This is the rule of common law and of the New York penal code, which defines as manslaughter the killing of one human being by the act, procurement, or omission of another, without design to effect death, by a person engaged in committing or attempting to commit a misdemeanor affecting the person or property, either of the person killed or of another.

In 1844 the case of Rice *v*. The State (8 Mo., 561) was decided in Missouri. Rice, a Thomsonian, undertook by the same methods used on Lovett to cure Mrs. Keithley of sciatica. She had not been so well for years as when he began to treat her, and was within six weeks of giving birth to her fourth child. Under his system she fell into premature labor and died within about ten days. He was convicted of manslaughter; but the appellate court, adopting the rule in Thomson's case, the facts being substantially the same, reversed the judgment.

In 1881 another case arose, in Iowa, State *v*. Schulz (55 Ia., 628). Schulz treated a sick woman by acupuncture and an irritating oil, according to the system of Herr Baunscheidt, who, having been much benefited by the bitings of small insects, sought to give the world, for a consideration, a simulacrum of his experience. Defendant admitted that he did not know the composition of the oil, that being Baunscheidt's secret. The patient died. Schulz claimed that if he had not been interfered with he could have helped her, and produced twenty-three witnesses to testify that Baunscheidtismus, as administered by him, had benefited them. Schulz was convicted, but the appellate court reversed the judgment, following the cases of Thomson and Rice, and expressed this conclusion: "The interests of society will be subserved by holding a physician civilly liable in damages for the consequences of his ignorance, without imposing upon him criminal liabilities when he acts with good motives and honest intentions." The adoption of this theory by the New York statute of 1844 enabled quackery, in the words of Beardesley, J., to "boast its triumphant and complete establishment by law" (Bailey *v*. Mogg, 4 Den. 60). And the people of Iowa, instead of adhering to it, have passed, since the Schulz case, a law forbidding medical practice to be unlicensed.

Notwithstanding these acceptances of the rule in Thomson's case by other jurisdictions as sound law, the Supreme Court of Massachusetts, wherein it originated, has since held, in

Commonwealth *v.* Pierce (138 Mass., 165, A.D. 1884), that the accuracy of its report was doubtful and its law open to criticism. The facts in Pierce's case were these: Defendant held himself out as a physician. There was no more law in Massachusetts to prevent him from so doing in 1884 than there had been to prevent Thomson's like pretension in 1809. Being called to a sick woman, he caused her, she consenting, to be kept for some three days swathed in flannel underclothing saturated with kerosene. Under this treatment she died in great misery. There was evidence in the case that in some instances similar treatment by defendant had resulted favorably, but also that in one it had burned and blistered the flesh, as in the case of deceased. Defendant's counsel at trial asked the court to charge, following the rule in Thomson's case, that defendant could not be convicted unless it were proven beyond reasonable doubt that death resulted from his treatment, and that he had such knowledge or probable information of the fatal tendency of his prescription as to justify the jury in presuming that death was the effect of his obstinate or wilful recklessness, and not of an honest intent and expectation to cure. This request was refused, defendant was convicted, and his conviction affirmed by the appellate court, who, by Holmes, J., said that the language of Thomson's case relied upon by defendant—viz., that "to constitute manslaughter the killing must have been a consequence of some unlawful act. Now there is no law which prohibits any man from prescribing for a sick person, with his consent, if he honestly intends to cure him by his prescription"—was ambiguous and wrong, if it meant "that killing must be the consequence of an act which is unlawful for independent reasons apart from its likelihood to kill." "Such," continued the court, "may once have been the law; but for a long time it has been just as fully, and latterly, we may add, much more willingly, recognized that a man may commit murder or manslaughter by doing otherwise lawful acts recklessly, as that he may by doing acts unlawful for independent reasons, from which death accidentally ensues." Thomson's case, it was said, did not intend to lay down new law, but cited and meant to follow Lord Hale, whom it had taken too literally, since his lordship admitted that other persons might make themselves liable by reckless conduct (I. P. C. 472); and why not a physician as well?

As to what constitutes criminal recklessness in such cases, the court said substantially that the standard is not gauged by the actor's belief or idea of danger, but by common experience. If the thing done "is generally supposed to be universally harmless and only a specialist would foresee that in a given case it would do damage, a person who did not foresee it and who had no warning would not be held liable for the harm. . . . The use of the thing must be dangerous according to common experience, at least to the extent that there is a manifest and appreciable chance of harm from what is done, in view either of the actor's knowledge or of his conscious ignorance. . . . Common experience is necessary to the man of ordinary prudence, and a man who assumes to act as the defendant did must have it at his peril. . . . The defendant knew he was using kerosene. The jury have found that it was applied as the result of foolhardy presumption or gross negligence, and that is enough. . . Indeed, if the defendant had known the fatal tendency of the prescription, he would have been perilously near the line of murder." The rule laid down in this carefully reasoned case must commend itself to prudent men; for it really amounts only to this: that if one unversed and unskilled in medical science and practice undertakes, nevertheless, the cure of a patient, and in so doing uses remedies or adopts a treatment—whether positive or negative ought to make no difference—from which there is a manifest and appreciable chance of harm according to common experience, he shall be held liable for his recklessness and shall not be excused by the innocence of his intention. And certainly when part of the treatment adopted is the exclusion of proper treatment, this is just as harmful as if positively injurious methods were adopted. It is just as much homicide to cause death by starvation by keeping food from the victim as to use an active poison.

How does this principle apply to "Christian Science," "faith cure," or any eccentric treatment of the sick—not excluding voudoo or the "scandal cure" *—that by operating

---

* I knew once of a malade imaginaire who for years had drifted feebly from bed to lounge and back again. Physicians were in vain. One day a friend called and said that the newspapers had gotten hold of a bit of history that would interest the nation on the following Sunday. The patient leaped from the lounge, took a cab to the steamer office, and by Sunday was on the ocean. This is the "scandal cure."

strongly on the mind may restore the lost equilibrium?   Is the pursuit of any of these methods "practice of medicine"?

While the ordinary quack, who, as has been said, pretends only to extraordinary human skill or knowledge, is therefore generally held to be a practitioner of medicine, Christian Scientists, who go further and pretend to procure for lucre divine intervention by their prayers, contend that in thus offering to heal the sick, although for hire, they are not practising medicine, but observing religious rites, and are therefore protected in their practices by constitutional safeguards.   We are thus brought to consider what is the "practice of medicine." The answer to this query must depend in most instances upon the words of the statute and the peculiar circumstances of the case.   In the New York case of Smith *v.* Lane (24 Hun, 632, A.D. 1881), plaintiff, apparently a masseur, sued for agreed fees which defendant refused to pay on the ground that plaintiff, not being licensed to practise medicine, could not recover compensation for his treatment, which, as the opinion of the court recites, "consisted entirely of manipulation with the hand.   It was performed by rubbing, kneading, and pressure." The court said:

"The practice of medicine is a pursuit very generally known and understood, and so also is that of surgery.   The former includes the application and use of medicines and drugs for the purpose of curing, mitigating, or alleviating bodily diseases; while the functions of the latter are limited to manual operations, usually performed by surgical instruments or appliances. . . . To allow incompetent or unqualified persons to administer or apply medical agents, or to perform surgical operations, would be highly dangerous to the health as well as the lives of the persons who might be operated upon, and there is reason to believe that lasting and serious injuries as well as the loss of life have been produced by the improper use of medical agents and surgical instruments or appliances.   It was the purpose and object of the Legislature by this act to prevent a continuation of deleterious practices of this nature, and to confine the uses of medicine and the operations of surgery to a class of persons who, upon examination, should be found competent and qualified to follow these professional pursuits. *No such danger could possibly arise from the treatment to which the plaintiff's occupation was confined.   While it might be no ben-*

efit, it could hardly be possible that it could result in harm or injury.

"And for that reason no necessity existed for interfering with this pursuit by any action on the part of the Legislature. It may be that credulous persons would be deceived into the employment of the plaintiff, and in that manner subjected to imposition. But it was no part of the purposes of this act to prevent persons from being made the subjects of mere imposition."

Either the italicized words are superfluous or they contain an implication that if the treatment, in the court's opinion, had been capable of causing injury like improper medical treatment, the judges would have classified it in the same category.

In Eastman *v.* State (10 N. E., 97), an Indiana case, the court said, on the other hand: "It is the purpose of the statute to prevent persons who do not possess the necessary qualifications to practise medicine or surgery from inflicting injury upon the citizens by undertaking to treat diseases, wounds, and injuries." And again: "The State has an interest in the life and health of all its citizens, and the law under examination was framed, not to bestow favors upon a particular profession, but to discharge one of the highest duties of the State—that of protecting its citizens from injury and harm." In People *v.* Phippin (70 Mich., 6), the defendant was held to have practised medicine, on proof that he held himself out as "Dr. W. W. Phippin, magnetic healer," had attempted to cure the sick, and in the case of a child's death had certified the cause to be "canker, sore mouth. Duration of disease: June 3 to July 22, 1887." In Bibber *v.* Simpson (59 Me., 181), a clairvoyant who gave remedies was said to be practising medicine. So also in Nelson *v.* Harrington (72 Wis., 591). And in New York, De Leon, who prescribed for a child, drawing its horoscope and giving some rhubarb, was convicted of illegal practice of medicine. The administration of electricity has also been held to constitute medical practice—Davidson *v.* Bohlman (37 Mo. App., 576).

The Ohio statute provides that "Any person shall be regarded as practising medicine or surgery, within the meaning of this act, who shall append the letters M.D. or M.B. to his name, or for a fee prescribe, direct, or recommend for the use of any person any drug or medicine or other agency for the

treatment, cure, or relief of any wound, fracture, or bodily
injury, infirmity, or disease." That seems very broad; but in
the case of Eastman v. State (6 Ohio Dec., 296), it was held,
in January, 1897, that a "graduate of the school of osteopathy
of Kirkville, Mo.," was not practising medicine by kneading
and manipulations, using only his hands and no medicines.
The court cited Smith v. Lane, and held that the words, "any
other agency," were too vague and were limited by the particular words, "drug or medicine." *

The New York statute does not define medical practice.
Such a definition was framed in the draft of the act of 1887,
but stricken out because a certain Senator, who died shortly
afterward, declared that it would include an eccentric healer
who had saved him from the grave. The definition was yielded
to save the bill.

The Nebraska medical act defines as a practitioner any one
"who shall operate on, or profess to heal, or prescribe for, or
otherwise treat any physical or mental ailment of another."

Under this statute arose, in 1894, the case of State v. Buswell (40 Nebr., 158). The defendant, charged with unlawful
practice of medicine, claimed to be a Christian Scientist, graduated from the Metaphysical College of Mrs. Mary B. G. Eddy,
of Boston. Defendant offered testimony to cures wrought by
him in cases of rheumatism, rattlesnake bite, pneumonia, and
scarlet fever—the last in the case of a child four years old.
He testified that in eighteen months he had treated about one
hundred persons, of whom only two had died. The accuracy of
his diagnosis was not in issue. He testified that the text-books
of the Christian Science Church are the Bible and Mrs. Eddy's
work, "Science and Health." He denied that in a medical
sense he treated physical or mental ailments, saying: "I understand with God's laws, and not mortal man's." Questioned
as to the privilege of patients or parents to call in medical
aid, he said: "We believe that every one has a right to express
their wish, and it is always understood that if they prefer some
other treatment, or some other mode, or some one else to aid
them, it is their privilege. We always do that. It is taught
in our text-books. We never give any medicine; that is entirely contrary to the teaching of Christian Science." And

* But the contrary was held in Illinois. See Eastman v. State, 71 Ill.
App., 236, cited on the Brief in this pamphlet.

this counsel said: "The defendant, and those of the same faith with him, believe as a matter of conscience that the giving of medicine is a sin; that it is placing faith in the power of material things, which belongs alone to Omnipotence. To the Christian Scientist, it is as much a violation of the laws of God to take drugs for the alleviation of suffering or the cure of disease, as for a Methodist clergyman to take the name of his God in vain to relieve his overwrought feelings."

Being asked if he took pay from his patients, he said: "As a rule I do not. We tell them we leave the question to them and God. . . . Jesus says the laborer is worthy of his meat, and we expect that those whom we spend our lives for to remunerate us for it. If they are not willing to part with the sacrifice themselves, it is not expected that those should reap the benefit." Considering that defendant described his treatment as one of prayer, this intimation that the answer to prayer would be contingent on the payment of the Scientist's fee apparently seemed rather blasphemous to the court, who very aptly cited two cases from one of the science's text-books, the Bible—the former, that of Simon the sorcerer (reported in Acts viii. 18–23), to whom Peter said, "Thy money perish with thee, because thou hast thought that the gift of God may be purchased with money"; the second, that of Gehazi (2 Kings v. 20–27), servant of Elisha, who, finding that his master had gratuitously cured of leprosy Naaman, the rich Syrian, thus establishing a precedent for dispensary abuses, remarked, "As the Lord liveth, I will run after him, and take somewhat of him," and in the end took not only a fee, but the disease. Upon these precedents the Nebraska court ruled thus:

"The exercise of the art of healing for compensation, whether exacted as a fee or expected as a gratuity, cannot be classed as an act of worship. Neither is it the performance of a religious duty, as was claimed in the District Court." They further said: "The object of the statute is to protect the afflicted from the pretensions of the ignorant and avaricious, and its provisions are not limited to those who attempt to follow beaten paths and established usages." This, it will be noticed, is very different from the view of the New York law taken in the New York case of Smith *v*. Lane and the Ohio case of Eastman *v*. State (*supra*), as well as from the latest case of the kind, State *v*. Mylod (40 At., 753), decided in Rhode Island last July upon these facts: Defendant undertook to cure one Hale of malaria and one Vaughan of grip, by apparently engaging in silent prayer and giving them pamphlets on Christian Science. He received a fee of $1, but gave no medicines, made no examination or diagnosis. He testified that he did not attempt to cure disease, had no knowledge of medicine or surgery, and that his only method was "prayer and effort to encourage hopefulness for all who come to him in public or private, and whatever diseases they imagine they have." The court held, citing Smith *v*. Lane, that in the absence of diagnosis, prescription of remedies, or surgical methods there was no medical practice. They suggested that if Christian Science is practice of medicine, then as a school it is entitled to recognition by the State Board, and that it would be absurd to hold, under the Rhode Island statute which forbids discrimination against medical schools, that requirements could be prescribed which members of a particular school could not comply with, since that would be not to discriminate only, but to prohibit.* And the court distinguished the cases of clairvoyant physicians upon the ground that therein the defendants had prescribed medicine and professed to cure diseases. There seems to be fallacy in the implication by the court that any educational requirements as a condition of medical license are prohibitory upon any persons except those who are unable to acquire an education; and it is quite proper to exclude such persons from the ranks of physicians.

The question is full of difficulty. Every one admits the power of mental impulses in nervous diseases; admits nature's healing force that so often cures without any attendance at all; and admits that it would be wrong to forbid all recourse to any aid. But this much being conceded, are we to admit also that any person should be entitled to take charge of the sick merely because he pretends to act under religious beliefs and to abstain from using those remedies and methods arrived at by study and investigation? Are we to punish the physician who fails to report yellow and scarlet fevers, diphtheria, and other contagious disorders, and allow a person who boasts his ignorance of medical and sanitary science to treat and conceal such cases? The Christian Scientist, in his madness or worse, says

* On this point cf. Dowdell *v.* McBride, 45 S. W. 397, cited on the Brief in this pamphlet.

that there is no disease but only fear or loss of relation to God, which he in his blasphemy undertakes to restore, providing he is paid for his services. What, then, would his death certificate be? Would it be that Jones was permanently scared? What would his report of a contagious disease be? That Brown has a panic, which is likely to spread?

In the case of Reynolds *v.* United States (98 U. S., 145, A.D. 1878), the Supreme Court of the nation applied common sense to this proposition, that the name of religion may be used to cloak either lust or imposture. Defendant, a member of the so-called Church of Jesus Christ of Latter-day Saints, being indicted for bigamy, pleaded in defence that the penalty imposed by his church upon its male members who failed to practise polygamy "when circumstances would admit" was "damnation in the life to come." No such dreadful penalty hangs over a Christian Scientist who abstains from his lucrative practices. The Supreme Court said in Reynolds' case: "Laws are made for the government of actions; and while they cannot interfere with mere religious belief and opinions, they may with practices." Can it be seriously contended, asks the court, that a civilized nation may not lawfully suppress human sacrifices and the Indian custom of suttee, because their votaries claim religious sanction therefor; or polygamy for the same reason? To suffer such things, it was answered, "would be to make the professed doctrine of religious belief superior to the law of the land, and in effect to permit every citizen to become a law unto himself. Government could exist only in name under such circumstances." These wise words of the court apply even to honest believers, whom we may respect, or, at least, sympathize with, even in their delusions. But if the defence of religion were allowed to the extent that the eccentrics claim, the deadly sin of lying would become even more prevalent than it is, and the dangerous classes would go over in a body to *soi-disant* religion.

There was an English case in 1868, Reg. *v.* Wagstaffe (10 Cox's Cr. Cas., 530), wherein parents were charged with manslaughter of a child because, pursuant to their religion as members of the "Peculiar People," they neglected to provide medical attendance for it, in a case of acute inflammation of the lungs; instead they anointed and prayed over it. The court charged that if they had let the child starve for want of food, the case would have been different; for every one recognizes the need of food. But it was not the same when the question was one of medical attendance, for as to that opinions differed, and he read to the jury from the general Epistle of St. James (v. 14, 15) those words upon which the Roman Church rests the doctrine of extreme unction, and the Mormons and " Peculiar People " rest their doctrine of healing the sick by anointing and prayer only; words which the learned and sensible commentator, Adam Clark, forcibly argues to be an exhortation by the Apostle to use the ordinary Eastern remedy, oil, as well as prayer, in treating the sick.   The jury acquitted. Recently in a like case, Reg. v. Cook, they disagreed.*

Beyond doubt there are very honest, intelligent, cultivated persons who believe in the efficacy of Christian Science and faith cure.   Among some twenty cases of death under such treatment, including cases of contagious diseases, the writer has noted the names of such persons.   It is equally true that some "intelligent persons" find no "fad" too extraordinary for adoption.   The writer knew of a most shrewd and cultivated woman who consulted in Sing Sing prison as to investment in stocks an "astrologer," convicted not only of illegal medical practice, but of abhorrent crime.   It is said that where voudooism prevails, cultivated people consult its priestesses, after the fashion of Nicodemus.   And when St. John Long, prince of quacks, was convicted of manslaughter at the Old Bailey (4 Car. and P., 398) among the twenty-nine patients who testified to the excellence of his treatment were divers "ladies of quality," headed by the Marchioness of Ormond, than whom, save royalty, only a duchess could be better able to form a sound opinion in such case.

But nothing is more false than to say that medical laws forbid the practice of Christian Science, faith cure, voudoo, vitapathy, or any other "pathy" or cult.   Those laws provide only, at most, that no person shall practise medicine who has not pursued a course in medical study.   There is nothing in

* This case should have been cited as Regina v. Senior, the conviction in which was affirmed after this article appeared (*Law Times*, December 17, 1898 ; vol. cvi., p. 151).   The decision apparently is made under the Act for the Prevention of Cruelty to Children (57 and 58 Vict., ch. 41, 10). In Cook's case the jury found the parent guilty of gross negligence, but could not or would not agree that the negligence was the proximate cause of death (see letter to *Medical Record* of January 21, 1899).

them to prevent any licentiate from practising as he pleases. There is nothing to prevent a masseur without license from washing and rubbing a man, if he confines himself to that. But there is no reason why unqualified persons should be allowed to pretend to cure disease, by their pretenses deprive the sick of the benefits of science, and yet escape the just consequences of their imposture. The whole case of these people who desire to earn a livelihood by treating the sick without any adequate preparation therefor through study and investigation was summed up in the grotesque falsehood, circulated by way of petition to the New York Legislature of 1885 for the repeal of the medical law, which said:

"The law deprives from practising in this State persons who are gifted with the power of healing by the laying of hands, through the presence and imparting of vital magnetic force, and otherwise. Some of these powers are natural to the practitioner, and cannot be imparted or increased, but are likely to be limited or impaired by the course of study required by medical colleges." Could anything be more absurd? The natural power to heal disease impaired by the acquisition of knowledge concerning disease! And yet there were those prepared to believe even that, so true is it to-day, as of old, that the wonderful is the unknown and the credible that which is impossible of belief.

It may be a question of policy whether Christian Scientists should be prosecuted; whether cheap martyrdom might not strengthen them. But there seems no good reason, as matter of law, why they should not be punished for the evil they actually do; prohibited, if the policy seem wise, from treating the sick without adequate preparation by study of medical science, and convicted of manslaughter if death results from interference.—*From the "Medical Record," Nov. 26th, 1898, by permission.*

INSANITY.

Its Classification, Diagnosis and Treatment;

A Manual for Students and Practitioners of Medicine.

BY

E. C. SPITZKA, M. D.,

Professor of Medical Jurisprudence and of the Anatomy and Physiology of the
Nervous System, at the New York Post-Graduate School of Medicine, President of the New York Neurological Society, etc.

In this, the first systematic treatise on Insanity published in America since the days of the immortal Rush, the author has made its definitions, classifications, diagnosis and treatment plain and practical ; and has laid particular stress upon points comparatively new and has succeeded in presenting the subject in such a manner that the rudiments of this difficult and intricate branch of medicine may be easily acquired and understood.

☞ This important work has already been adopted as the *Standard Text-Book* in the College of Physicians and Surgeons of New York, the College of Physicians and Surgeons of Baltimore, the Rush Medical College of Chicago, the College of Physicians and Surgeons of St. Louis, and the Medical-Chirurgical College of Philadelphia.

The Boston Medical and Surgical Journal says: "Conservative and in accordance with the highest principle of scientific investigation, which accepts no half-truth, but proven facts alone. . . . Its chief merit consists in its effort to present the subject in a clear, accurate, and scientific manner."

The Louisville Medical News says: "The book is written in a clear and forcible style, and while the practical side of the question is kept constantly in the foreground, it abounds in incidents, historical and modern, which admirably illustrate the points made by the author, and contribute largely to the entertainment of the reader."

The Weekly Medical Review says: "It cannot be neglected by any one desiring a clear and comprehensive review of the whole subject of insanity."

The New York Medical Record says: "The accomplished author displays throughout a masterly grasp of his intricate subject, and a familiarity with its bibliography which is in the highest degree commendable. . . The presentation of his arguments is direct and decided, his illustrations usually apt and well put, and his expositions of the most important points forcible."

The Cincinnati Lancet and Clinic says: "A great variety of useful information and an intelligent discussion."

The American Medical Weekly says: "It is clear, it is up to the times, and last but not least, it is practical."

The New England Medical Monthly says: "By far the best book that has appeared in English in this department of Science."

In One Large Octavo Volume, 424 pages. Illustrated. $2.75.

E. B. TREAT & CO., 241-243 W. 23d St., New York.

ILLUSTRATED SKIN DISEASES.

AN ATLAS AND TEXT BOOK

WITH SPECIAL REFERENCE TO MODERN DIAGNOSIS AND THE MOST APPROVED
METHODS OF TREATMENT.

By WILLIAM S. GOTTHEIL, M.D.,

Professor of Skin and Venereal diseases at the New York School of Clinical Medicine; formerly Lecturer on
Dermatology in the New York Polyclinic; Consulting Dermatologist to the Orphan Asylum of the
Sheltering Guardian Society; Dermatologist to the Lebanon Hospital, the North
Western and the West Side German Dispensaries; Fellow of the New
York Academy of Medicine, and Member of the New
York County Medical Society, etc.

The pictorial representation of disease is a recognized aid to the practitioner in every department of medicine; but in Dermatology it is of pre-eminent importance. In the study of skin diseases, the great majority of the symptoms are objective and visual, and the diagnosis must be made by the eye-sight alone. It is very difficult to represent in words the manifold impressions and the delicate variations of color and shape that are so readily appreciated through the optic nerve.

It is not surprising, therefore, that the attempt to depict on paper and preserve permanently the varied and evanescent forms of skin diseases has occupied the attention of many Dermatologists. Yet it can hardly be claimed that a degree of success commensurate with the efforts made has been attained; which is largely due, of course, to the necessary limitations' of the methods employed. Photography gives us form; but color, an element of equal importance in depiction, is absent. It can rarely be done from life by the anatomical artist, and when possible, entails an expense that is almost prohibitive; it can never be as delicately minute as Nature is. Chromo-lithography at best is more or less crude, since it is an attempt to imitate the varying tints and shades of nature in a few striking colors by mechanical processes.

In this combined Atlas and Text-book of Skin Diseases the colors are as true as the forms, since both are obtained through the camera. The vast strides made in *color-photography* during the last year or two have rendered it possible to produce a series of life-like representations. The artist's brush has not been used, and the color plates are made from color negatives directly taken from living subjects. *Additional features are:*

1. The introduction into the text of a large number of illustrations in black and white, made, for the most part, from negatives taken of the author's own cases drawn from his extensive hospital, dispensary and private practice, and made under his immediate supervision.

2. The few necessary anatomical and pathological illustrations are mostly photo-micrographs; made with the camera from actual section.

3. The great advances made in Dermato-therapeutics, and the modern methods of treatment are fully recognized.

CONDITIONS.—The work will be issued in **Quarto Portfolios,** each comprised of four colored plates of cases from life, 24 quarto pages of descriptive and profusely illustrated text with numerous *formulæ.*

---

13 portfolios. Each, $1.00. Bound in half morocco, $15.00.

E. B. TREAT & CO., 241-243 West 23d Street, New York.

A SYSTEM OF
LEGAL MEDICINE

A Complete Work of Reference for Medical and Legal Practitioners.

By ALLAN McLANE HAMILTON, M.D.,
Consulting Physician to the Insane Asylums of New York City,

——ASSISTED BY——

LAWRENCE GODKIN, Esq., of the New York Bar,

And a Corps of Thirty Collaborators

In its various departments, with which their scientific reputation is identified.

THE list of contributors to this great work includes the names of some of the most distinguished writers and authorities upon Medical Jurisprudence in America. As a book of reference it will be found an invaluable help to medical men and by those of the legal profession who desire the aid of the most advanced and sound opinions of practical students of forensic medicine. So much opprobrium has been attached to the word "expert," that the spirit which so often impels men to go into Court and become ardent partisans, finds no place in this system, and it will be the aim of the Editor and his Colleagues to give the work a decided judicial and impartial tone, so that it may be consulted with confidence by all as an authority of the first order.

Until recently the contributions in the United States to the literature of Medical Jurisprudence have been exceedingly meagre, if we may except Beck's classical but antiquated treatise, and other works limited in scope. For some time it has been the fashion to consult Foreign books which are written for the benefit of trans-Atlantic readers, and in many respects are inapplicable to our methods, and not in conformity with the legal usages of this country. We therefore believe that the appearance of an American treatise of this character will be especially timely and welcome.

A feature of the book will be the introduction of short articles upon special subjects prepared by distinguished members of the American Bar which will form appendices to the different articles.

The legal gentlemen, who have been invited to write articles upon subjects with which they are especially familiar, have in most instances acted in conjunction with a medical collaborator.

The Editor has aimed to make the work under consideration a repository of the most advanced ideas and valuable cases, and, except when the latter are unique, indispensable, or especially pertinent, it will be his aim and that of his associates to avoid threadbare material, and to illustrate the articles by new examples. The scope of the work is necessarily very great, but it is trusted that its contents will be found to be practical and concise. Extraneous matter is dispensed with, and the reader will be spared dry and uninteresting details and valueless decisions. A feature of "Hamilton's System of Legal Medicine" will be the presentation of a large amount of new experimental research.

THE WORK will be comprised in two large royal octavo volumes, of about **700 pages each**; illustrated when practicable and desirable by Photographic reproductions from Nature and other Drawings and Special Diagrams; by Chromo-lithography and Engravings in line and half-tone process.

THE MECHANICAL EXECUTION—paper, press-work and binding—will be equal to the best known to the art of book-making.

In Substantial Cloth Binding, per volume, - $5.50

In Full Sheep, Uniform Law Style, per volume, 6.50

SOLD BY SUBSCRIPTION. Orders taken only for the complete work.

Descriptive 32-page Pamphlet, giving List of Contributors, Synopsis of Contents, Specimen Pages, etc., etc., **sent on application.**

E. B. TREAT & CO., 241-243 West 23d Street, New York.

TREAT'S MEDICAL CLASSICS.

Octavo volumes, uniform in size and style of binding (Cloth), $2. each.

SYNOPSIS OF THE PRACTICE OF MEDICINE.
For Practitioners and Students. An embodiment of the late *Systems* and *Cyclopædia*. By WM. BLAIR STEWART, A.M., M.D., Lecturer on Therapeutics, and late Instructor in Practice of Medicine Medico-Chirurgical College, Philadelphia.

CLINICAL DIAGNOSIS.
By ALBERT ABRAMS, M.D., Professor of Pathology, Cooper Medical College, Pathologist to the City and County Hospital, San Francisco. Third Edition.

MODERN GYNECOLOGY.
Comprising the latest treatment in this branch of Medical Science. By CHARLES H. BUSHONG, M.D., Assistant Gynecologist and Pathologist to Demilt Dispensary, New York.

DISEASES OF THE HAIR AND SCALP.
By GEORGE THOMAS JACKSON, M.D., Professor of Dermathology, Woman's Medical College, New York Infirmary; Chief of Clinic and Instructor in Dermathology, College of Physicians and Surgeons, etc.

INSANITY; A MANUAL OF.
Its Classification, Diagnosis and Treatment. By E. C. SPITZKA, M.D., Professor of Medical Jurisprudence of the Nervous System, New York Post-Graduate School. Second Edition.

NERVOUS EXHAUSTION (NEURASTHENIA).
Its Hygiene, Causes, Symptoms and Treatment. By GEORGE M. BEARD, A.M., M.D., formerly Lecturer on Nervous Diseases in the University of the City of New York; Fellow of the New York Academy of Medicine, etc. Third Edition Revised and Enlarged by A. D. ROCKWELL, A.M., M.D., late Professor of Electro-Therapeutics in the New York Post-Graduate Medical School and Hospital, etc.

SEXUAL NEURASTHENIA.
Devoted to Genital Debility. Its Causes, Symptoms and Treatment, with a Chapter on Diet for the Nervous. By GEORGE M. BEARD, A.M., M.D. Edited by A. D. ROCKWELL, A.M., M.D. Fifth Edition.

EXCESSIVE VENERY, MASTURBATION AND CONTINENCE.
Their Etiology, Pathology and Treatment, including diseases resulting therefrom. By JOSEPH W. HOWE, M.D., late Professor of Clinical Surgery in Bellevue Hospital Medical College; Fellow of the New York Academy of Medicine; Visiting Surgeon to Charity and St. Francis Hospitals.

DISEASES OF THE NOSE AND THROAT.
By P. WATSON WILLIAMS, M.D., M.R.C.S. (London), Physician in charge of Throat Department, Bristol Royal Infirmary; Honorary Physician to the Institute for the Deaf and Dumb.

SURGICAL HANDICRAFT.
A Manual of Surgical Manipulations, and Minor Surgery. By WALTER PYE, F.R.C.S., Surgeon to St. Mary's Hospital and the Victoria Hospital for Sick Children, of Glasgow. Revised and Edited by T. H. R. CROWLE, F.R.C.S., Surgical Register to St. Mary's Hospital, and Surgical Tutor and Joint Lecturer on Practical Surgery in the Medical School.

8vo. 600 pages. Fully illustrated. Cloth, $3.50 net; Sheep, $4 net.

E. B. TREAT & CO., 241-243 West 23d Street, New York.

www.ingramcontent.com/pod-product-compliance
Lightning Source LLC
Chambersburg PA
CBHW030540270326
41927CB00008B/1452

* 9 7 8 3 3 3 7 3 6 9 9 3 4 *